Cambridge Elements ≡

Elements in Eighteenth-Century Connections
edited by
Eve Tavor Bannet
University of Oklahoma
Markman Ellis
Queen Mary University of London

PARATEXT PRINTED WITH NEW ENGLISH PLAYS, 1660–1700

Robert D. Hume
Penn State University

CAMBRIDGE
UNIVERSITY PRESS

Shaftesbury Road, Cambridge CB2 8EA, United Kingdom

One Liberty Plaza, 20th Floor, New York, NY 10006, USA

477 Williamstown Road, Port Melbourne, VIC 3207, Australia

314–321, 3rd Floor, Plot 3, Splendor Forum, Jasola District Centre,
New Delhi – 110025, India

103 Penang Road, #05-06/07, Visioncrest Commercial, Singapore 238467

Cambridge University Press is part of Cambridge University Press & Assessment,
a department of the University of Cambridge.

We share the University's mission to contribute to society through the pursuit of
education, learning and research at the highest international levels of excellence.

www.cambridge.org
Information on this title: www.cambridge.org/9781009454124

DOI: 10.1017/9781009270502

When citing this work, please include a reference to the DOI 10.1017/9781009270502.

First published 2023

A catalogue record for this publication is available from the British Library

ISBN 978-1-009-45412-4 Hardback
ISBN 978-1-009-27051-9 Paperback
ISSN 2632-5578 (online)
ISSN 2632-556X (print)

Paratext Printed with New English Plays, 1660–1700

Elements in Eighteenth-Century Connections

DOI: 10.1017/9781009270502
First published online: December 2023

Robert D. Hume
Penn State University

Author for correspondence: Judy Milhouse, jmilhous@gc.cuny.ed

Abstract: This Element, *Paratext Printed with New English Plays*, has a lot to tell us about what playwrights were attempting to do and how audiences responded, thereby contributing substantially to our understanding of larger patterns of generic evolution across two centuries. The presence (or absence) of twelve elements needs to be systematically surveyed: (1) attribution of authorship; (2) generic designation; (3) performance auspices; (4) government license authorizing publication; (5) dedication; (6) prefaces of various sorts; (7) (a-b-c) list of characters (three types); (8) actors' names (sometimes with descriptive characterizations – very helpful for deducing intended authorial interpretation); (9) location of action; (10) prologue and epilogue for first production. Surveying these results, we can see that much of the generic evolution traceable in the later seventeenth century gets undone during the eighteenth – a reversal largely attributable to the Licensing Act of 1737. This title is also available as Open Access on Cambridge Core.

Keywords: paratext, Restoration drama, publishing history, censorship, title page elements

ISBNs: 9781009454124 (HB), 9781009270519 (PB), 9781009270502 (OC)
ISSNs: 2632-5578 (online), 2632-556X (print)

Contents

A Note from the Series Editors

Sadly, Rob Hume passed away, after a short and shockingly sudden illness, as this volume was going into production. Typically of his altruism and generosity of spirit, he had been working on a book about those he considered the leading critics of the twentieth and early twenty-first century. He surely belonged in such a book himself. No one has done more to reshape our understanding and appreciation of Restoration and Eighteenth-century theater, and more recently, of opera, than Rob. A committed historicist who believed that information and data are more useful to others than ideology and will certainly outlast it, he charmed librarians into finding all-but forgotten archives hidden in unopened cardboard boxes in library basements. He will be remembered for his brilliant and prolific scholarship – but also through the many lives he touched. Rob mentored, professionalized and supported generations of women students and women faculty. Many will mourn the loss with him of a true friend – a man of integrity and principle, of ruthless honesty and unbending loyalty, who cared, and could be relied upon for good advice and practical help in any emergency. It is an honor to have his work in our series, and we hope that he would have approved of the editing, copy-editing and formatting decisions we have had to make without him.

Eve Tavor Bannet, November 2023

Introduction

So far as I am aware, no one has ever systematically surveyed and analyzed paratext in the new plays that were professionally performed and then published in London between 1660 and 1700.[1] My subject is almost entirely first editions of plays newly written and performed after 1660, including the many plays that are substantive adaptations of pre-1642 drama. (George Buckingham's *The Chances* performed by 1664 and published in 1682, adapting John Fletcher's play of that title, performed 1615–25? and published in 1647 is a good example.) By my reckoning, such plays total some 377. The number cannot be exactly determined because in a few cases we do not know definitively that a published play was performed, and how much alteration is required to make a play "new" cannot readily be quantified. The title page is a given. It may or may not supply a subtitle and a generic descriptor. Usually, but not invariably, the title page names the playwright and states where or by whom the play was performed. After 1670, the Dramatis Personae often (though not always) records the name of the actor of each part. Beyond that, dedications, prefaces, imprimatur (government permission to publish, when mandated by law), identification of genre, prologue and epilogue, and specified "location" of the action (e.g., "London") are possibilities. "Agency" is often impossible to assign, and might be owing to playwright, bookseller, or printer – a problem I have not attempted to address.[2] And I have treated publishers' advertisements as outside the remit of this Element.

Paratext is a rich but not fully exploited resource for scholarship, and it will repay investigation. I need to make explicit up front that I am addressing two radically distinct audiences and must beg the indulgence of the reader when I seem to be bogged in bibliographic trivia (e.g., licensing dates), or alternatively soaring aloft to supply a 40,000-foot overview of generic evolution largely unconnected to evidence grounded in the physical book (which has disconcerted some bibliographers). The quantitative description and analysis of twelve kinds of paratext in 377 plays dated 1660–1700 ought, I believe, to be of assistance to bibliographers and editors dealing with those plays, but also to scholars and critics whose concern is with the evolution of English drama across two centuries circa 1600 to circa 1800. Paratext has a surprising amount to tell us about what playwrights attempted to do and how audiences responded. Letter and diary responses to plays are thin on the

---

[1] For anyone in need of some basic orientation in this relatively new and rapidly developing subfield, I would suggest consulting Genette (1997), Smith and Wilson (1997), and Erne (2013).

[2] The long standard and invaluable daily performance calendar helpfully reports some kinds of paratext, but not others. See Avery et al. (1960–8). On the rather problematic history of this important enterprise and its direly flawed index added to Avery by Ben Ross Schneider Jr. (1979), see Hume, "The London Stage, 1660–1800," in *The Electronic British Library Journal* (2022 articles).

ground and mostly rather subjective and slapdash. Newspaper and magazine reviews are largely nonexistent until the last third of the eighteenth century.

This Element had its origin in notes about norms and departures from those norms 1670–89 made for the benefit of the editors of plays in *The Cambridge Edition of the Works of Aphra Behn* (now starting to come into print). My original draft dealt exclusively with the last four decades of the seventeenth century, but readers kept asking how the plays of those decades "fit" with pre-1642 drama and led into eighteenth-century developments. The answers I have come up with seem to me usefully provocative of thought. I grant the unconventional nature of the enterprise. But beyond providing the late seventeenth-century particulars, I wish to demonstrate how paratext helps us (1) to understand the multifarious variety of English drama at any point in time, and (2) to trace the larger patterns of generic evolution across two centuries.

The Twelve Paratextual Elements

The twelve principal paratextual elements that I have identified and systematically surveyed across the 377 plays dated 1660–1700 are:

1. Authorial credit, usually on the title page (which is almost always dated by year), but occasionally only in a signed dedication. Anonymous publication dwindled fast.

2. Generic designation on the title page, usually following title (and frequently subtitle).[3]

3. Designation of auspices in a statement reporting performance by a particular company and/or at a specific theatre.

4. A government license authorizing publication, usually printed on the title page, when such licensing was mandated by law (1662–79 and 1685–95), but often omitted, the law notwithstanding.

5. A dedication (often with an extensive and sometimes gushy tribute).

6. Prefaces of various sorts, usually but not always by the playwright.

7. a.-b.-c. A list of the characters in the play. These come in three distinct forms, discussed in what follows.

---

[3] All plays are naturally published with a title, but subtitles become far more frequent after 1660. (Subtitles must be distinguished from *alternative* titles, which are much more common prior to 1642.) For the years 1631 through 1642, of 109 new plays professionally performed and published, 15 (14%) carried a subtitle and 94 (86%) did not. In the 1660s, of 68 new plays, 23 (34%) carried a subtitle while 45 (66%) did not. In the 1670s, of 125 new plays, 59 (47%) had a subtitle and 66 (53%) did not. In the 1680s, of 61 new plays, 38 (62%) had a subtitle and 23 (38%) did not. In the 1690s, of 123 plays, 57 (46%) had a subtitle and 66 (54%) did not. The cumulative figure for 1660–1700 is 377 plays, of which 177 (47%) had a subtitle and 200 (53%) did not.

8. The names of the performers in the first production. Exceedingly rare before 1642, and after the Restoration almost unknown until 1668, but after that identification of at least the principal actors and actresses rapidly became a standard though not invariable feature of play quartos.

9. A statement about the location of the action (abbreviated "Loc" in the data table), often placed at the end of the Dramatis Personae list, which, for example, in Congreve's *The Old Batchelour*, ends simply "The Scene, *LONDON*."

10. A prologue and epilogue written for the first production.

The evidentiary basis of this Element is the massive table that constitutes Appendix B ("Twelve Varieties of Paratext in 377 New English Printed Plays, 1660–1700"), in which I have attempted to record analytically the varieties of paratext to be found in every new play known to have been professionally performed and subsequently published in London between the reopening of the theatres in 1660 and 1700. The terminal date is somewhat arbitrary. Licensing of publication came to an end in May 1695, and the rest of the decade demonstrates considerable stability in publication practices. I will devote the remainder of this Element to analysis of the facts, figures, changes, and variety of what the data table can tell us. Much of this material is often ignored and omitted even in modern critical editions and almost always by editors of student texts and anthologies. By way of conclusion, I will briefly suggest that much of the generic evolution that paratext helps us trace in the seventeenth century is in fact largely undone in the course of the eighteenth century – a reversal that can be pretty decisively attributed to the Licensing Act of 1737.

The frequency of appearance of the twelve common types of paratext is summarized for each of the last four decades of the seventeenth century in Appendix A: "Cumulative Statistics by Decade and in Toto." Here I must issue a caution about the seeming exactitude of the figures. The features to be found in any particular copy of a seventeenth-century edition can easily be tallied. The playwright's name is on the title page, or it is not. The quarto contains a prologue and an epilogue, or it does not. Unfortunately, not all copies are identical. For example, three states of the first edition of Aphra Behn's *The Rover* (1677) exist, all three printed for John Amery, with the author's name on only one of them (Folger copy B1763b). A second example is the two states of the title page of George Digby's *Elvira*, both illustrated on Early English Books Online (EEBO). One state, ESTC R232462 (Wing 4764), has no license and an imprint with the unusual spelling for the publisher as "Henry Broom" (illustrated by the Newberry copy on EEBO). The other, ESTC R9341 (Wing B4764A), wrongly calling it "Anr Edn," has the license by Estrange dated 15 May 1667 and the correct spelling "Henry Brome" (reproduced on EEBO from a Huntington copy with frontispiece portrait of Digby). Allardyce Nicoll and *The London Stage* report only that with a licensing date.[4] Such minor but sometimes significant variances are a fact of life and must be allowed for. A third example is Henry Cary's (?) *The Mariage Night* (pub. 1664), where the license appears at the end of the prelims. I could easily have failed to spot a license that appeared in an unusual location – or the EEBO copy may lack a license present in other copies.

The examination of the primary evidence has been carefully done and checked, but the evidence is not totally uniform, and judgment sometimes comes into play. Consider the issue of "characters described" in a Dramatis Personae list. This important component of paratext varies greatly from playwright to playwright, and it changes over time. I have tried to indicate variation by employing delimiters (e.g., "Some" and "A bit"). I have counted these instances as "Yes" if the first edition "describes" at least some of the characters for the reader – but another scholar might exclude a very incomplete case. I have dithered over some generic categorizations. And I have agonized over some attributions, frequently resorting to "(?)" when reporting long-standing attributions for which I consider the evidence inadequate. I report what the first edition says or fails to say, but where a later attribution seems definitive, I record that [in brackets] for the reader's convenience, while noting that it is lacking in the first edition. I have also had to report some half a dozen cases in which standard and long-unquestioned attributions appear to me to have no satisfactory basis.

Background

Most paratext was published in the prelims of late seventeenth-century play quartos, which appeared as singletons.[5] Reprints were almost always in quarto, in most cases verbatim, and comparatively infrequent.[6] In the late seventeenth century, play quartos were a standard product at a standard price (usually 1*s*). Following 1660, remuneration arrangements for playwrights underwent a drastic change that scholars did not fully recognize and confront until 2015.[7] Prior to 1642, playwrights generally sold their scripts outright to acting companies,

---

[4] Nicoll (1965), 1:403. *The London Stage*, Part 1, p. 95. The editors may, of course, simply have copied Nicoll.

[5] Early in the period, a few members of the nobility and gentry preferred to publish multi-play folios, notably the Earl of Orrery, Sir Robert Howard, and Sir William Killigrew. Retrospective collections of works of Thomas Killigrew and Sir William Davenant appeared as massive folios in 1664 and 1673 respectively, the latter posthumously.

[6] These established norms were to change with astonishing rapidity between 1714 and 1718, when octavo replaced quarto as the nearly universal choice for first editions of plays, and duodecimo became the norm for reprints. On these changes, see Milhous and Hume (2015), chapter 2.

[7] See Milhous and Hume (2015), pp. 43–45.

ceding both performance and publication rights in perpetuity for a flat fee agreed
upon by the contracting parties (though a benefit performance was sometimes part
of the agreement). After 1660, remuneration for perpetual acting rights became
the profit (if any) of the third night if the play lasted that long in its first run.[8] But
in compensation for loss of the traditional cash-on-the-barrelhead fee for performance rights, playwrights were allowed to sell publication rights (in perpetuity) for whatever a bookseller might be willing to venture on a particular play.[9]

I bring up the sale of publication rights here because it raises issues concerning
the origin and content of the script to be published. In the absence of typewriters,
computers, and electronic transmission, much paratext depended on the precise
source, nature, and content of the handwritten manuscript delivered to the printer.
Timing also needs to be taken into consideration. The gap between premiere and
publication changed radically over the last four decades of the seventeenth
century.[10] For many years, twentieth-century scholars followed Allardyce
Nicoll in believing that the gap was a month or two. Item-by-item analysis
shows, however, that in the 1660s, the gap varied but was usually something like
six months to a year (and sometimes substantially longer). In the 1670s, the time
lapse shrinks, falling to a norm of about three months. In the troubled time of the
Popish Plot and the Exclusion Crisis, the gap becomes wildly variable. Three
months remains normal, but six- and eight-month gaps are not uncommon.
Around the beginning of the 1690s, the standard gap abruptly becomes about
a month, or even less. A probable reason for this is regime change. The licensing
law did not officially expire until 3 May 1695, but for most practical purposes, it
was not really enforced after William III's arrival on the throne in 1688. Thereafter,
whether for reasons involving protection of the right to copy or the growing
realization that spectators in the theatre might well prove the likeliest purchasers
of the printed text, publication almost always followed closely on first performance.

After 1660, the source of the manuscript set by the printer must usually have
been the playwright. If the "gap" was three months or more and the play had
enjoyed whatever run it achieved, perhaps the MS prompt copy could be borrowed
for use by the printer.[11] Or the author might have retained an advanced draft,
personally have copied a quasi-final draft, or paid a prompter's clerk to make
another copy. At some point, someone had to assemble dedication, preface, or other

[8] A second benefit was added by 1690 (sixth night); later, a third was also added (ninth night).
[9] For details of all known cases of benefit income and sale of copyright in 1660–1800, see Milhous
and Hume (1999) and *The Publication of Plays* (2015), Appendix I.
[10] On the changing time lapse and suggested redatings for some forty-five plays, see Milhous and
Hume (1974).
[11] On demonstrable use of promptbooks as copy for the printer, see Langhans (1981), pp. xiv–xv.
Langhans points out that we often cannot be sure that a given note or stage direction in
a promptbook is authorial.

prefatory matter (if such items were to be included), prologue and epilogue, and names of the actors (if added to the Dramatis Personae). Printing of text proper almost invariably begins with the B gathering.[12] Evidently, the printer often started there and could wait a while for the arrival of the paratextual material that would populate the A gathering.[13] The order in which such elements, when present, appear in the prelims varies, but I will survey them in the most common order.

Ten Varieties of Paratext and Two Subsets

Comparative statistics for each of the twelve categories, decade by decade and in toto, may be found in tabular form in Appendix A.

(1) *Authorial Credit* (column 1 of Appendix B). The norm was to identify the author by name, which overall occurred fully 85% of the time, usually with genre specified if not obvious from the title. The exception is the mid- and later 1680s, when identification of the playwright rises to 95%. The reason seems clear. After the union of 1682, the managers of the United Company decided that with no competition, they need bother to mount no more than three or four new plays a year.[14] Quite naturally they accepted almost nothing not written by established professional playwrights (whose names on title pages possessed value) or company insiders. In the six years 1677–82, the two companies had staged eighty-five new plays, or about fourteen per annum. In the six years 1683–8, the United Company staged just twenty-three, or about four per annum.

At the other extreme, no playwright might be named. The reasons for anonymity evidently varied. A grandee like the Duke of Buckingham probably felt that publishing was for lesser beings; there is no evidence that he had any hand in the publication of *The Chances* (eighteen years after its premiere) or *The Rehearsal*. Both appeared in print with no hint of authorial origin and little paratext beyond auspices, prologue, and epilogue.[15] Aphra Behn signed most of her plays (though not all of those extensively based on old plays), but even in the late 1690s, other women playwrights tended to be coy (e.g., *She Ventures, and He Wins*, "Writen by a Young Lady," pub. 1696). Some of the plays "seen to the stage" (and thence into print) by such actors as William Mountfort and George

---

[12] A very rare exception is the first edition of Aphra Behn's *The Rover* (1777) in which I.i. commences on A4r. Normal practice would have been to print the epilogue there if space permitted – which it did. I have no explanation for this anomaly.

[13] Claire Bowditch reminds me of a passage in Aphra Behn's preface to *The Luckey Chance* (pub. 1687) in which she refers to precisely this situation: "Had I a Day or two's time, as I have scarce so many Hours to write this in (the Play, being all printed off and the Press waiting)."

[14] Another factor was acquisition of rights to all plays owned by the defunct pre-1642 King's Company, which included almost all pre-1642 drama. On the radically unequal division of rights to Elizabethan, Jacobean, and Caroline plays when the theatre revived in 1660, see Hume (1981).

[15] The 1682 edition of *The Chances* did not even have a list of characters, which was extraordinary.

Powell in the eighties and nineties were probably written by amateurs happy to oblige their actor friends without seeming to stoop to ungentlemanly pursuits. After the 1660s, knights and lords mostly refrained from playwriting, which had rapidly become an enterprise dominated by professionals.

Interestingly, though playbills appear to have exercised significant influence on the content of title pages, the reverse seems much less true. (Too few playbills survive from before 1700 to permit a conclusive generalization.) Main title, subtitle if any, and very often genre are duly picked up by publishers. In the 1660s, 82% of the published plays identify the author, usually on the title page. (That number fluctuates, but the overall figure for the whole forty-year period is, coincidentally, 82%.) But if Dryden is to be believed, and I think he is, never until 1699 did a playwright's name appear on a playbill. Writing to Mrs. Steward on 4 March 1698[/9], he says: "This Day was playd a reviv'd Comedy of Mr Congreve's calld the Double Dealer, which was never very takeing; in the play bill was printed, – Written by Mr Congreve; . . . the printing an Authours name, in a Play bill, is a new manner of proceeding, at least in England."[16] One might suppose that the playwright's name would help attract an audience, at least in the case of proven professionals, but repertory theatres tended to be pretty conservative, and the managers were extremely slow to adopt this innovation. Of course, new plays in the theatre were anonymous prior to publication except by rumor among cognoscenti, so audience members might have good associations with a successful play without knowing who wrote it. Publishers soon learned to take advantage of such knowledge. The title page of the first edition of Aphra Behn's *Sir Patient Fancy* (1678), for example, declares that the play was "Written by $M^{rs.}$ A. Behn, the Authour of the *ROVER*." A lot of people must have seen and enjoyed that very popular play without encountering Behn's name in connection with it. Latter-day scholars need to understand that for seventeenth-century readers of books, authorship of plays had become paramount by mid-century, but for theatre-goers, that became true much more gradually over the next several decades.

(2) *Generic Designation on the Title Page*, with or without attribution (reported in column 2 of Appendix B; absence indicated by *). (For an example, see Behn's *Rover*, Folger copy B1763a.) This convention seems designed to assist potential readers browsing in bookshops. In this respect seventeenth-century title pages anticipate the practice found in eighteenth-century playbills and newspaper bills, which usually contain genre descriptors.[17] A genre designation would of course have been a convenience to a manager or script reader, especially in years when

---

[16] Dryden (1942), pp. 112–113. Claire Bowditch points out to me that known holdings of early playbills are too late and scanty to allow us to determine at what date they began to identify author via the "By the Author of . . . " formula.

[17] On playbill practice, see Vareschi and Burkert (2016).

a theatre was doing ten or more new plays and was presumably offered substantially more than that number. Generic designations are sometimes worked into titles (which I have counted as generic identification) – for example, Nathaniel Lee's *The Tragedy of Nero* (1674) or Thomas Durfey's *The Comical History of Don Quixote* (1694). The proportion of genre designations is 81% in the sixties, 87% in the seventies, 89% in the eighties, and 94% in the nineties. The reasons for not specifying genre evidently vary. Sometimes the title or subtitle makes the designation supererogatory (e.g., Joseph Harris's *Love's a Lottery*, 1699, or Lee's *The Rival Queens, or the Death of Alexander the Great*, 1677). In other cases, I deduce that the playwright was deliberately signaling a departure from generic norms. As instances I offer Dryden's *The Conquest of Granada* (two parts, 1670–1) and Thomas Southerne's *The Disappointment: A Play* (1684). For decade by decade and cumulative figures on genre descriptors, see Table 1. We can only guess who or what caused a change from state to state or edition to edition. The first state of Behn's *The Rover* (1677) says merely: "*The Rover. Or, The Banish't Cavaliers*." The second state adds "A Comedy" before proceeding to "Acted at His Royal Highness the Duke's Theatre." The third adds: "Written by Mrs. A Behn."

The 32 "Other" cases break down as follows. Farce: 8.[18] Opera: 11 (though sometimes also labeled "Tragedy"). Masque: 1. Pastoral: 3. "Play": 6. "Novelty": 1. Musical: 2.

(3) *Designation of Auspices* – a statement along the lines of "As it is Acted at the Theatre-Royal, By His Majesty's Servants" (title page of Southerne's *Oroonoko*, 1696). Presence of such a statement is indicated by †, absence by ⊥, in Appendix B, column 2. Professional performance in London was regarded as enhancing a book's appeal, and the company/venue statement is to be found on the title page of almost every play entitled to make the claim. Of the 377 plays in the Appendix Table, 357 make such a claim on the title page (see Plates 1, 2, and 3), 17 do not, and in 3 cases, the EEBO copy is defective and fails to supply a title page. But of the 17 "No" cases, 14 precede 1670 and 11 precede the closure of the theatres on account of plague in June 1665. The scattered later cases strike me as flukes. Ravenscroft's adaptation of *Titus Andronicus* was not published until more than five years after its premiere. The cast was not named, and the original prologue and epilogue were lost. The omission of the venues for Durfey's *The Campaigners* and *III Don Quixote* was probably just due to someone's inattention.

---

[18] Given the substantial number of plays in the late seventeenth-century repertory that might legitimately be dubbed "A Farce," the rarity of that descriptor seems interesting. Claire Bowditch points out to me that the original title page of Behn's *The False Count* (1682) blatantly so labels it ("*A FARCE Call'd The False Count*"), but the prominent descriptor disappears in the cancellans version of the play's title page.

Table 1 Genre descriptors

Decade	No. of plays	Comedy	Tragedy	Tragi-comedy	History	Other	None
1660s	68	32 (47%)	14 (20.5%)	9 (13%)	1 (1.5%)	0	12 (18%)
1670s	125	53 (42.4%)	43 (34.4%)	4 (3.2%)	2 (1.6%)	6 (4.8%)	17 (13.6%)
1680s	61	22 (36%)	16 (26.2%)	3 (5%)	1 (1.6%)	11 (18%)	8 (13.1%)
1690s	123	56 (45%)	41 (33%)	3 (2.5%)	2 (1.5%)	15 (12%)	6 (5%)
Totals	**377**	**163 (43.2%)**	**114 (30%)**	**19 (5%)**	**6 (1.6%)**	**32 (8.5%)**	**43 (11.5%)**

Clearly, by the end of the 1670s, the "auspices" statement was utterly standard. It comes, however, in a bewildering number of variants. Either company (King's, Duke's, Their Majesties Servants) or theatre (Lincoln's Inn Fields, Drury Lane, Dorset Garden) might be named, or a combination thereof. Examples are "As it is Acted at The Duke's Theatre" (Ravenscroft's *London Cuckolds*), "As it is Acted by His Majesties Servants" (Crowne's *City Politiques*), and "As it is Acted by Their Majesties Servants at the Queens Theatre in Dorset Garden" (Jevon's *The Devil of a Wife*). Ambiguity sometimes arises in the era of the United Company (1682–94), which used both Drury Lane and Dorset Garden (though so far as we know never on the same day), but surviving evidence suggests that what was staged at Dorset Garden tended to be opera and plays requiring fancy stage machinery.

(4) *Government License Authorizing Publication* ("Lic" in column 8 of Appendix B). In principle and under law, licensing for publication was required for all sorts of books and pamphlets, plays included, between 10 June 1662 and March 1679, and again after the accession of James II in 1685 (in a law taking effect on 24 June 1685) until its final collapse effective with the prorogation of Parliament on 3 May 1695.[19] The license usually takes the form of a statement on the title page (occasionally elsewhere in the book) such as: "Licensed, 3 June 1676. Roger L'Estrange" (title page of the 1676 first edition of Etherege's *The Man of Mode*). But by my reckoning, of the circa 230 plays in this table that ought to have borne such a license, only 80 (35%) actually do so.[20] I can offer no satisfactory explanation.

Plays were also licensed for performance, an entirely separate matter. We know quite a lot about the process (though less than we would like to in some respects). Sir Henry Herbert was the licenser for performance until his death in 1673.[21] He was followed by Thomas Killigrew, who gave place to his son Charles in 1677.

---

[19] For a sane and helpful account of the relevant licensing laws, see Treadwell (2002). For a detailed elucidation of the struggle over regulation of the press circa 1679 and 1680, see Crist (1979), apparently unknown to Treadwell. On the final collapse, see Astbury (1978).

[20] A related issue, non-paratextual but relevant, is the requirement that publishers enter their claims to copy in the Stationers' Register – an obligation stipulated not by the government, but by the company's rules and honored largely in the breach. In principle, a publisher's claim to each of the 377 plays ought to have been entered in the company's register (and a fee of 6d paid). But item-by-item examination shows that in the 1660s, 37 of 68 plays were entered in the Register (54%); in the 1670s, 28 of 125 (22%); in the 1680s, 8 of 61 (13%); and in the 1690s, 5 of 123 (4%), with none at all after 1691. That many of the plays of the period 1660–1700 were not entered in the register is a well-known fact (the actual total was 78 of 377 or about 21%), but scholars (with the notable exception of D. F. McKenzie) have almost unanimously tiptoed around that fact rather than acknowledging it and puzzling over it. Why publishers bothered to enter the titles they did (and pay the fee) is by no means clear. I have been unable to discern any correlation between what got licensed and what got entered in the Stationers' Register.

[21] For an excellent and too-little-used edition of Herbert's surviving records, see Bawcutt (1996). For a still useful account of the operations of that office, see White (1931).

Little direct evidence or testimony has survived, but so far as we know, *every* new play performed by the patent companies in London between 1661 and 1715 was duly vetted by the Master of the Revels.[22] Very few manuscripts survive bearing the censor's objections and deletions. The fee was two pounds per script, which does not sound like much until one remembers that this amounted to one-twentieth of the average annual household income in England at the time.[23]

Much less is known about the fees, modus operandi, and results of Sir Roger L'Estrange and other licensers for print. A pair of striking examples will illustrate this point. In 1682, Shadwell published *The Lancashire Witches* with extensive passages printed in *italics* to identify matter not permitted by the Master of the Revels in performance. Eighteen years later, Colley Cibber published the complete text of *The Tragical History of King Richard III*, including the entirety of Act I, which had been deleted from the performance text by the Master of the Revels, who claimed it might call for sympathy for James II, exiled since the Revolution of 1688.[24] I am aware of no contemporary remarks on the oddity of this discrepancy concerning these or other instances. What could not be said on stage could be put in print absolutely legally for all to ponder, accompanied by the aggrieved playwright's bitter complaints.

(5) *A Dedication* (indicated by "Ded" in column 8 of Appendix B). This was in no sense obligatory, but quickly became a feature of a large number of plays. They are least common in the 1660s (only 29% versus 61% for the four decades as a whole). The reason seems obvious: a fulsome dedication was a de facto appeal for a pecuniary reward, but in the 1660s, many of the new plays were written by lords, knights, and fine gentlemen aspiring for reputation, not income. Of the sixty-eight new plays staged in that decade, eleven were written or coauthored by Dryden and Shadwell (not counting Dryden's contribution to the *Tempest* adaptation of 1667), but they were the only playwrights we regard as professional dramatists, and they were just starting to learn their trade. Dedications are immensely varied. Many merely express sycophancy or personal friendship, but some are serious critical or aesthetic justifications for the work that follows. Boasting of success is common, but so is lamentation of failure in the theatre. Reasoned explanations of the playwrights' choices are fairly rare, but sometimes helpful. Dryden's dedications and prefatory matter are exceptionally rich in substantive commentary.[25]

---

[22] On the collapse of licensing after Sir Richard Steele received his patent in January 1715, see Milhous and Hume (1987). Censorship was of course restored by Sir Robert Walpole's Licensing Act of 1737 and not repealed until 1968.

[23] See Hume (2014).

[24] Cibber complains at length in his preface to the first edition (1700) and continued to seethe for the next forty years. See his account of the episode in *An Apology for the Life of Mr. Colley Cibber* (Cibber 1889).

[25] On which see Hume (1970).

(6) *Critical Apparatus*. The line between "dedications" and "prefaces" or related notes "To the Reader" and the like is often blurry or even nonexistent. Their presence in a play quarto is recorded under various descriptors in column 8 of Appendix B.[26] Looking at some of Dryden's efforts in these realms, I might point to "A Defence of an Essay of Dramatique Poesie, Being an Answer to the Preface of [Sir Robert Howard's] *The Great Favourite, or the Duke of Lerma*," which prefaced *The Indian Emperour* (1667); "Of Heroique Playes," preface to *The Conquest of Granada* (1672); the preface to *Troilus and Cressida* (1679), which contains an extensive essay on "The Grounds of Criticism in Tragedy," running together to some 10,000 words of fairly technical critical argumentation; and the preface to *An Evening's Love* (1671), which offers some 4,000 words of very detailed analysis of what "comedy" can be and should try to do. Twentieth- and twenty-first-century scholars have made little (and often condescending) use of late seventeenth-century criticism, which exists largely as prefatorial paratext. Some of it is superficial or self-serving, but there is a lot of meaty, substantive information about what the playwrights were attempting to achieve.[27]

(7.a.b.c.) *Three Varieties of Lists of the Characters' Names*. A "Dramatis Personae" list had long been a standard feature of pre-1642 plays and remained the norm for new plays in the 1660s. Throughout the four decades at issue, 98% of new plays carried a list of the Dramatis Personae, often under that designation.[28] Unsurprisingly, the lowest percentage was in the 1660s – still a very substantial 96% (sixty-five out of sixty-eight plays). The key question was what information would be conveyed beyond a simple list of names. The three basic variants are:

a. A list of names of the characters (e.g., Bayes in Buckingham's *Rehearsal*), with presence (Yes) or absence (No) noted in column 4 of Appendix B.
b. A list of the characters' names, plus explanation of their "connections" (son of, wife of, daughter of, his friend, the Queen's Eunuch, etc.), with presence (Yes) or absence (No) of such explanation noted in column 5 of Appendix B, often with the names of the performers specified.
c. A list of names, plus connections, plus "characterization" with presence (Yes) or absence (No) noted in column 4 of Appendix B – for example, Heartwell in Congeve's *The Old Batchelour*, "a surly old Batchelour, pretending to slight

---

[26] Commendatory poems by friends or bigwigs are relatively rare and seem to me to fall in a separate category. Where present, I have called attention to them in footnotes. I count only thirteen instances, all but four of them from the 1690s.

[27] For a useful overview, see Cannan (2006).

[28] Some writers evidently had personal preferences. Dryden was fond of "Persons Represented" and Wycherley invariably used "The Persons." When the performers' names are supplied, "The Actors Names" is sometimes employed, as in Otway's *Friendship in Fashion* – but not always, as evidenced in Buckingham's *Rehearsal* (1672). See Plate 4.

Women; secretly in Love with *Silvia*." These sometimes extend to considerable detail, often, but by no means always, with the names of the performers added.[29]

Explanation of the connections amongst the characters was very much the norm: overall 85%. "Characterization" in the Dramatis Personae list was far less common. By my reckoning it was a mere 26% (eighteen of sixty-eight cases) in the 1660s, and never topped 50% in the seventeenth century. I offer the speculation that the increase in characterization reflects growing concern with readers, especially readers outside of London who might never see the play. Characterizations are almost certainly not aimed at the actors. Playwrights usually helped cast the play, they read the script aloud at the start of rehearsals, and they often assisted in direction.[30] An actor who wanted explanation of his or her character could usually ask the playwright.

(8) *Listing the Names of the Performers against Their Roles*, with presence (Yes) or absence (No) noted in column 7 of Appendix B. A fourth variant on the Dramatis Personae page was to start with any of the first three, adding the name of the performer of each role (or at least the major roles).[31] The first post-1660 plays published with the actors' names were Sir Robert Stapylton's *The Slighted Maid* and *The Step-Mother*, both performed in 1663 and published in 1663 and 1664, respectively. The innovation evidently attracted no notice. But in 1668, three plays were published with cast specified. They were Orrery's *History of Henry the Fifth* (performed in 1664), Orrery's *Mustapha* (performed in 1665), and Dryden's *Secret-Love* (performed in 1667). For the 1660s, the figures as a whole are 20 of 68 plays published with the names of the actors (29%), but by 1670, naming the performers had become more common than not. The figures for the seventies soared to 79 of 125 (63%), and they reached 81% (100 of 123) in the nineties.

I cannot recall any scholarly commentary on lack of printed casts in play quartos for most of the 1660s. I confess that until now I had never thought much about this rather significant gap, or the rapid arrival at a new norm at the end of that decade. The reason for this obliviousness, I conjecture, is that we possess fairly full casts for about forty plays in the 1660s because John Downes printed them in his *Roscius*

---

[29] For example, Sir William Belfond in Shadwell's *The Squire of Alsatia* (1688): "A Gentleman of above 3000*l. per annum*, who in his Youth had been a Spark of the Town; but married and retired into the Country, where he turned to the other extreme, rigid, morose, most sordidly covetous, clownish, obstinate, positive and froward." The present-day reader needs to understand that £3,000 in 1688 had a quite fantastic buying power. By MeasuringWorth.com's conservative retail price index calculator, the buying power today would be some £530,000.

[30] For a discussion of casting and rehearsal practices in the later seventeenth century, see Milhous and Hume (1985), chapter 2.

[31] Printing the cast with the text of a play prior to 1660 was a rarity. Gerald Eades Bentley's Appendix of "Casts and Lists of Players" in the *Profession of Player in Shakespeare's Time* reports only some twenty cases.

Anglicanus (1708).[32] Fifteen of those casts were for King's Company plays (old and new), the rest mostly post-1660 new plays staged by the Duke's Company, in which Downes served as prompter. Adding Pepys's copious commentary on performers between 1660 and the cessation of his diary in 1669, we can legitimately feel that we have a decent grip on the "lines" and fortes of many early Restoration performers. Pepys's massive diary (nine volumes of text plus a volume of commentary and a volume comprising an index) is much quoted but in fact remains seriously underutilized as a primary source to be mined by theatre historians.[33]

Exactly what precipitated the sudden alteration in the norms of play publication we can only guess, but how the change came about is easy to explain. Stapylton's *The Slighted Maid* was "Printed for Thomas Dring" in 1663, and his *The Step-Mother* was "Printed by J. Streater; And are to be sold by Timothy Twyford" in 1664. I deduce that the innovation was brought about by Stapylton (perhaps wishing to curry favor with the actors?), even if it had no immediate impact. But if we look at the three plays that appeared in 1668 with printed casts, we find a common factor, or perhaps two. In all three cases, the book was "Printed for H. Herringman," who dominated play publication in the first fifteen years after the Restoration. Herringman was a trend setter and other publishers followed his lead. The fact that two of the plays were by Orrery may well be significant. Whether the earl was being gracious or politic we can only guess, but he seems likelier to have suggested adopting Stapylton's innovation than the still relatively junior Dryden.

I cannot overstress the importance of naming the performers for the modern interpreter of these plays. Playwrights very often wrote with particular performers in mind. To cast the manly and heroic Charles Hart as Horner in Wycherley's *The Country-Wife* does not suggest that fornicator was being harshly satirized (as many modern critics have believed). To cast the large, fierce, intimidating John Verbruggen as Mr. Sullen in Farquhar's *The Beaux Stratagem* makes his physical threats to his wife upsetting, not comic (Verbruggen played Iago to Betterton's Othello). Casting one of the company's clowns in that part would have produced a radically different effect. The failure of almost all major modern editions to annotate cast lists when present and to analyze their implications for interpretation is shocking.[34] I see the rapid growth in identification of performers that started in 1668 as clear evidence that the relatively small, increasingly knowledgeable Restoration audience was able to imagine the named performers in a play, even if they had not yet attended a performance (and perhaps never would).

---

[32] Downes (1987), pp. 4–66.   [33] Pepys (1970–83).

[34] I have developed this argument at some length in "Annotation in Scholarly Editions of Plays: Problems, Options, and Principles," in *Notes on Footnotes: Annotating Eighteenth-Century Literature*, ed. Melvyn New and Anthony W. Lee. Penn State Series in the History of the Book (Pennsylvania State University Press, 2023).

(9) *Location for the Action Specified* (e.g., "London," or "Bohemia," or "Dover"). If present, this labeling is usually found at the end of the Dramatis Personae, though specific changes of setting within the play are customarily signaled act by act or scene by scene as appropriate. A general setting ("Location" as I am terming it) is specified in roughly three-quarters of late seventeenth-century plays, a practice consistent throughout the period. If made explicit, "Loc" appears in column 8 of Appendix B.

(10) *Prologue and Epilogue*. Performances of new plays were invariably accompanied during the initial run by a purpose-written prologue and epilogue, delivered by a popular actor or actress. They were sometimes separately printed for sale at the time of premiere and were almost always included in the first and subsequent editions.[35] If present in the first edition, "P/Ep" appears in column 8 of Appendix B. They contain often valuable information about the dates of the plays, their content and aims, current events, and audience attitudes, though topicality can make them difficult to decipher or annotate. Fortunately, the monumental seven-volume Danchin edition collects them all, offers dating information when necessary, and supplies annotation that greatly assists the reader in navigating his or her way through what is often a blizzard of topicalities and local references.[36] Anyone using material from prologues or epilogues needs to consult his edition.

Lack of prologue and epilogue in a play quarto is highly unusual for a professionally performed play. Behn's (?) *The Revenge* (1680), an adaptation of Marston's *The Dutch Courtesan* (1605?), is a rare instance. Behn apologizes for the lack of a prologue in her *The Dutch Lover* (1673), saying in her address to the "Reader" that it is "by misfortune lost." Publishers who found themselves short of this bit of paratext sometimes resorted to the expedient of repurposing text filched from an old and probably mostly forgotten play. Diana Solomon has kindly pointed out some examples to me. The second, unspoken prologue to [Duffett's?] *The Amorous Old Woman* (1674) was reprinted as the prologue to Durfey's *The Fool Turn'd Critick* (1676) and then again as the prologue for Orrery's *Mr. Anthony* (1669 but not published until 1690). And the epilogue to Durfey's *The Fool Turn'd Critick* (1676) reappears as the prologue to his own *Injur'd Princess* in 1682. The epilogue to Lee's *Lucius Junius Brutus* (1680) turns up as the epilogue to Mrs Pix's *The Czar of Muscovy* (1701). Elaine Hobby suggests that I note the slightly dizzying case of Aphra Behn's posthumous *The Widdow Ranter* (perf. 1689; pub. 1690). Dryden wrote the prologue and epilogue used in performance, which were published separately by Tonson at the time of performance. But when Knapton published the play in quarto in 1690, the prologue supplied was what Dryden wrote for Shadwell's *A True Widow* (1678), of which Knapton had published the second

---

[35] On which see Wiley (1940). For analysis of their content and rhetoric, see Solomon (2013).
[36] Danchin (1981–8).

edition in 1689, and the epilogue was one lifted from the *Covent Garden Drollery* (1672). "Gallants you have so long been absent hence" was apparently written for a revival circa 1671–2 of Fletcher and Massinger's *The Double Marriage*, very possibly by Behn, and used by Behn as the prologue for her adaptation *Abdelazer* in 1676 (pub. 1677).[37] Danchin makes the plausible suggestion that the substitution of old work for what Dryden had supplied for performance was the result of disagreement over copyright and fee between Tonson and Knapton.

One occasionally encounters oddities with some interest and significance. A good example is the "Postscript" added to Part 1 of Aphra Behn's *The Rover* in which some copies have the added phrase "especially of our sex" although the Prologue refers to the author as "him."

Observations, Reflections, and Questions

Pondering the implications of the figures tabulated in Appendix A (drawn from the raw data in Appendix B), I want to offer some comments and questions in several realms.

I. *Continuity and Change*. Most drama scholars (especially "Renaissance" drama scholars) long assumed that the closure of the London theatres in 1642 created a radical break, and that when theatres were reopened in late 1660, a brave new world (or perhaps merely a degraded one) had begun. This view was seriously challenged as long ago as 1936 in an important but mostly disregarded book by Alfred Harbage.[38] He maintained that between 1626 and 1669, English drama evolved in an essentially unbroken continuum that included the Interregnum. Studies of post-1660 drama tended to jump quickly past the 1660s in order to concentrate on major plays by Wycherley, Etherege, Dryden, and Shadwell in the 1670s. Allardyce Nicoll's rather superficial and mechanical six-volume *A History of English Drama 1660–1900* aside, accounts of "Restoration" drama (mostly comedy) published in the 1950s and 1960s dealt with no more than about fifteen plays in toto.[39] When scholars finally got around to systematic analysis of genre evolution that took account of *all* of the plays performed in the London patent theatres, they found that the plays of the 1670s are very different in many respects from those of the 1660s.[40] The number of new plays professionally performed in London between 1660 and 1710 is circa 500 (counting both

---

[37] On this tangled history, see the account in Danchin (1981–8), 4:758–765.

[38] Harbage (1936). For a more extensive investigation of the form and content of Interregnum plays, see Randall (1995).

[39] Nicoll's *History* remains valuable for its exhaustive lists of plays and for its appendixes of documents, but its critical take on the plays themselves is embarrassingly simplistic.

[40] See particularly Hume (1976) and Hughes (1996). Hume is primarily concerned with generic characteristics; Hughes is much more oriented to ideology and content. The books are in fact complementary.

published and lost), and there is quite a lot of variety and change if one looks beyond the tiny canon celebrated by mid-twentieth-century critics.

Let me ask a blunt question: what does paratextual evidence have to tell us, if anything, about continuity or disjunction between 1642 and the 1660s? We may usefully inquire into the degree of solo authorship, collaboration, and anonymityin the early and later seventeenth century. Granting that what appears to be "solo" authorship may conceal collaboration (for example, the Duke of Newcastle did not thank his collaborators in print, but anecdotal evidence suggests that he received substantial professional help with his plays and compensated his helpers generously), and that anonymity may conceal collaboration, the figures available to us seem interesting.[41] I take the figures from Paulina Kewes's admirable account of the changing nature of playwriting in the course of the late seventeenth century.[42] Let us first consider two periods in their entirety, 1590–1642 versus 1660–1700.

Table 2 Solo-authored, collaborative, and anonymous plays, 1590–1642 versus 1660–1700

Period	Solo	Collaboration	Anonymous	Total
1590–1642	436 (52%)	170 (20%)	231 (28%)	837
1660–1700	361 (86%)	16 (4%)	42 (10%)	419

Table 3 Solo-authored, collaborative, and anonymous plays, 1631–42 versus 1660–70

Period	Solo	Collaboration	Anonymous	Total
1631–42	127 (83.5%)	9 (6%)	16 (10.5%)	152
1660–70	79 (82%)	8 (8.5%)	9 (9.5%)	96[43]

---

[41] "Collaboration" and "anonymous" often take us into fraught territory. Demonstrable reality is sometimes radically different from what title pages tell us or fail to tell us. Worse, we often have no evidence from which to verify or modify what a title page tells us. Only two post-1660 title pages announce a collaboration per se – Dryden and Lee's *Oedipus* (1678) and their *The Duke of Guise* (1682). The front matter of the Dryden–Davenant adaptation of Shakespeare's *Tempest* (pub. 1670) explains their collaboration. Extensive testimony makes clear that "Buckingham's" *The Rehearsal* (1671) was a committee enterprise, though it was published anonymously. And three of the Duke of Newcastle's plays were understood at the time to have benefited extensively from professional help (from Dryden on *Sir Martin Mar-all* and from Shadwell on *The Humorous Lovers* and *The Triumphant Widow*).

[42] Kewes (1998), Appendix A.

[43] By comparison, I note that my figures for 1661–70 are fifty-five (81%) attributed – of which I reckon four as collaborative – and thirteen (19%) anonymous, for a total of sixty-eight. But Kewes was counting *all* plays (including lost plays and those surviving only in manuscript), whereas I am tabulating paratext in printed plays.

The much smaller number of plays post 1660 is attributable to the Killigrew and Davenant patent grants of 1662 and 1663, which limited the number of theatre companies to just two. In the earlier period, the norm was multiple companies simultaneously. Across the whole of the 110 years at issue, there was obviously a huge swing toward single-author playwriting and a pronounced move away from collaboration and anonymity. The categories are inevitably a bit smudgy. Many of the anonymous plays were probably solo-authored, but we have potent evidence that some of the anonymous plays were in fact joint or group enterprises. "Buckingham's" *The Rehearsal* (1671) is an excellent example of the latter. But as far as paratext from title pages goes, evidence for collaboration exists for just *two* cases over the whole forty years. Late seventeenth-century title pages are an extremely incomplete and unsatisfactory source of statistics on collaboration.

If, however, we look not at the whole span of more than a century, but instead at the periods of roughly a decade immediately before and after the Interregnum, we get a different picture. Kewes's figures for those two subperiods run as follows:

In terms of the proportions of solo composition, collaboration, and anonymous publication, the percentages seem decidedly congruent, both between the 1630s and 1660s, and all plays versus published plays.

II. *New Developments in the 1670s.* Why should major generic developments have started to occur rather swiftly in the 1670s?[44] And how does paratext help us recognize and trace those changes? I see two reasons. First, a new generation of professional playwrights flourished with innovative confidence after getting their work staged at the end of the previous decade. Dryden's first play reached the stage in 1663, and he had seen seven more to the stage by the end of 1670 (including a collaboration with the Duke of Newcastle, but not counting his collaboration with Davenant in revising *The Tempest*). Shadwell's first play was staged in 1668 (*The Sullen Lovers*), and he had added three more by the end of 1670. Aphra Behn saw her first play to the stage in 1670; John Crowne, Elkanah Settle, and William Wycherley in 1671 (Wycherley admittedly more a gentleman than a professional); Edward Ravenscroft in 1672; Nathaniel Lee and Thomas Otway in 1675; Thomas Durfey in 1676; John Banks in 1677; and Nahum Tate in 1678. Several of them contributed significantly to the boom in titillating sex comedy that moved English comedy into new territory in the 1670s. These professionals were a new generation, writing for theatres that employed sexy women as performers. And scattered among their dedications, prefaces, and addresses (whether triumphant or grumpy) to readers, and

---

[44] For a useful array of contemporary comments exhibiting changing audience generic preferences in the 1670s, see Maguire (1992), chapter 4.

prologues and epilogues are all sorts of explanations that collectively help us understand the playwrights' aspirations for innovation (and some frustrations). A century before newspaper reviews started to become common and, in a world where "reception" was largely undocumented, authorial paratext is our best source of information about playwrights' aims and audience response.

A second factor that surely contributed substantially to generic change was a growing audience that needed to be accommodated with enlarged auditoriums.[45] The reader of paratext gets useful glimpses of the changing, growing audience, especially in the prologues and epilogues addressed to that audience. The 1661 "first" Lincoln's Inn Fields probably held circa 400 spectators; its successor Dorset Garden (opened in 1671) with vastly greater scenic capacity probably held circa 800 jam-packed.[46] I offer the hypothesis that when the King's Company built Drury Lane in 1674, they would have aimed at a similar capacity. We have no evidence that the number of courtiers doubled during the 1660s. Consequently, I deduce that the need for expanded auditoriums must have been created by a growing number of "cits" and bourgeois types – persons whose taste in plays was not necessarily identical to those of their social betters.[47] The post-1660 theatres were, of course, vastly more expensive to attend than their Shakespeare-era predecessors. The Restoration audiences were smaller and wealthier, but they were by no means socially or morally uniform.[48] We need to refrain from making easy assumptions about what particular segments of the audience would enjoy – or would not tolerate. No Carolean comedy ridicules the "cits" more vigorously or indecently than Ravenscroft's *The London Cuckolds* (1681). It remained frequently performed into the 1750s (mostly at Covent Garden), despite utter disdain on the part of the more genteel parts of the audience.[49]

III. *Licensing Puzzles*. Government licensing for both public performance of plays and printed matter of all sorts has been extensively studied, particularly the latter. Because most twentieth-century scholars regarded "censorship" with

---

[45] For a more extensive comparative discussion of early and late seventeenth-century auditorium capacity and prices, see the concluding "Overview" section of this Element.

[46] This actually represents a reduction in auditorium size from what twentieth-century scholars long assumed. For the traditional 1,200 figure, see Langhans (1972). A more sober set of estimates suggests capacity of circa 650 to circa 800. See Hume (1979) and (1982).

[47] Pepys comments on 2 January 1668: "Here a mighty company of citizens, prentices and others; and it makes me observe that when I begin [*sic*] first to be able to bestow a play on myself, I do not remember that I saw so many by half of the ordinary prentices and mean people in the pit, at 2*s*–6*d* apiece, as now; I going for several years no higher then the 12*d*, and then the 18*d* places."

[48] For the best published account of the composition of the Restoration audience, see Love (1980). By far the fullest account of the audience remains an unpublished Oxford D.Phil. thesis by Allan Botica (1985 [1986]) which runs to more than 400 pages. It is now dated in some ways, and it is an unrevised doctoral dissertation (Botica left academia), but it remains a useful resource.

[49] See, for example, the ferocious contempt heaped on the play in Baker (1764), I, under title.

hostility, much of the scholarship about the processes of licensing has been decidedly negative. Milton's *Areopagitica* (1644) has been hailed and the licencers regarded with scorn and contempt. But major puzzles need to be confronted in this realm.

This is not the place for a survey of the extensive scholarship that has been devoted to regulation of printed materials. For a recent, judicious, and helpful short overview, I strongly recommend the subsections on "Laws Regulating Publication, Speech, and Performance" in five chapters of Margaret J. M. Ezell's *The Later Seventeenth Century*.[50] What the laws said should happen and what actually occurred were two very different matters. The censors reportedly took bribes – not so much to issue a license as to overlook the lack of any license. The final collapse of the licensing process in 1695 has often been treated as a triumph for liberty of the press, but as Ezell points out, this is a simplistic and misguided interpretation. Inducing self-censorship can be a more efficient and effective means of achieving the desired results than paying a bevy of officials to scan a lot of texts before they are set in type. To cut a long story short, prepublication censorship yielded place to threat of post-publication prosecution for seditious libel.[51]

Preperformance censorship of plays carried out by the Master of the Revels worked erratically at best. In 1663, John Wilson's *The Cheats* received a license for performance, but was objected to after being performed and a pair of courtiers was directed to tidy it up.[52] Shadwell's *The Sullen Lovers* (1668) was, Pepys quickly learned, a blatant personal satire on Sir Robert Howard (as Sir Positive At-all) and his brother Edward Howard (as Poet Ninny), but any protests they may have made failed to halt either performance or publication. Plays banned because of allusion to the Popish Plot and the Exclusion Crisis circa 1682 were promptly allowed on stage in 1683 when the political situation had cooled off a bit – notably Dryden and Lee's *The Duke of Guise* and Crowne's *City Politiques*. In some respects, the most spectacular failure of theatrical regulation occurred after the publication of Jeremy Collier's *A Short View of the Immorality, and Profaneness of the English Stage* (1698). A flock of the plays that most outraged Collier continued to be a significant part of both companies' repertories (with the texts apparently unchanged), and the average purity of new comedies was little improved. Collier himself certainly did not believe that his diatribe and its follow-ups had succeeded in bringing about any improvement in the moral standards of new plays. Jonas Barish has argued that Collier's success made passage of Walpole's Licensing Act in 1737 "easy," but a rigorous examination of

---

[50] Volume 5 (1645–1714) in *The Oxford English Literary History*, pp. 33–40, 125–137, 252–264, 360–366, and 445–454.

[51] This is the subject of a recent and excellent book by Thomas Keymer (2019).

[52] On the details of this imbroglio, see Nahm's edition of *Wilson's The Cheats* (1935).

the old plays that remained in the repertory and the new ones mounted in the years after 1698 suggests, quite to the contrary, that Collier's near-total failure made eventual passage of Walpole's act "inevitable."[53]

Most scholars, myself included, now agree that the low percentage of entries for plays in the Stationers' Register (about 21%) reflects the rapidly declining authority of the guild toward the end of the century. Publishers' failure routinely to obtain a publication license for plays in the roughly twenty-six years when the licensing requirement was in force is much harder to understand. By my reckoning, only about a third of the plays that should have been licensed actually received one. Exactly what fees were due and collected by licensers for print is not altogether clear, and if publishers had a rationale for selecting those plays for which they actually bothered to obtain a license, I have failed to spot it.[54] Licensing for performance did have some demonstrable impact on what got performed and what the Master of the Revels excised, though we have no evidence of post-premiere regulatory oversight. Whether licensing for print had much impact on plays I am inclined to doubt.

IV. *The Importance of Performer Identification and Prefatory Criticism.* I want to underline both points. Twentieth-century editors and critics made dismally minimal use of this paratextual information. Casting often tells us a great deal about how a playwright conceived various roles. And comments in dedications and prefaces and addresses "To the Reader" often have a lot to say about degree of success (or lack of same) and what the audiences liked or disliked or failed to understand. Such paratextual material is often partisan, may be gloating or recriminatory, and is usually impossible to verify – but a century before reviews begin to become commonplace, it offers us some line on intention and reception.

V. *A Note on Post-1660 Reprints of Pre-1642 Plays.*[55] Surveying the changes in paratext norms in new plays between 1660 and 1700 invites a question: what impact (if any) did those norms have on reprints of pre-1642 plays that remained in or rejoined the active repertory? A rigorous investigation of those reprints is still needed. Many of them were in multi-play, usually single-author collections (generally not updated in any way), not singletons.

---

[53] See Barish (1981), chapter 8 (quotation at 235). For a detailed rebuttal of Barish's position, see Hume (1999b).

[54] For a still-useful account of the fierce disputes about licensing in the mid-1670s, see Kitchin (1913), chapter 7. By Kitchin's account, L'Estrange took bribes either to issue licenses or to ignore the absence of a license.

[55] For a convenient compendium on printed drama to 1642, the reader may wish to consult Berger and Massai (2014). This is the basis for a searchable digitization by Heidi Craig and Sonia Massai, hosted by the Folger Library, *Early Modern Dramatic Paratexts* (EMDP) (https://paratexts.folger.edu/About). I commend this valuable resource to the reader's attention.

But examination of some of the singletons reveals interesting variations. Six representative cases (taken in chronological order) will suggest some of the possibilities.

First, Jonson's *Catiline, As it is now Acted by His Majestie's Servants; at the Theatre Royal*. The title page states "The Author B.J." The 1669 edition has a newly written prologue and epilogue spoken by Nell Gwyn, includes a list of more than thirty-five "Persons of the Play," and specifies "The Scene, *Rome*." Actors are not associated with their parts, but a separate list is supplied of "The Principal Tragœdians" (Hart, Mohun, Beeston, Kynaston, and other current members of the King's Company). This was very much in the fashion of pre-1642 play publication, naming eminent members of the company but not specifying their parts in a particular play.[56]

Second, Beaumont and Fletcher's *A King and No King, As it is now Acted at the Theatre Royal, by His Majesties Servants* (1676).[57] Authorship is duly credited on the title page: "Written by *Francis Beaumont* and *John Fletcher*." Twenty-three characters are listed, together with the names of thirteen principal actors – current senior members of the King's Company, male and female. One part, very unusually, is given as "*Bessus* – Mr. *Lacy*, or Mr. *Shottrell*." When the play was reissued by Richard Bentley in 1693, it was pretty much verbatim, the cast included. The title page did replace "By His Majesties Servants" with "By Their Majesties Servants," but "As it is now Acted at the Theatre-Royal" was retained.

Third, *The Tragedy of Hamlet Prince of Denmark, As it is now Acted at his Highness the Duke of York's Theatre* (1676). "The Persons Represented" lists seventeen parts against the names of the performers – major and not so major members of the Duke's Company.[58] There was no prologue or epilogue, but one would not expect them. Prologue and epilogue were written for first runs and special occasions of various sorts, and this was simply a routine reprint of a repertory staple. But clearly the publishers (J. Martyn and H. Herringman) believed that currency and the names of the Duke's Company's players added sales appeal. They also tucked in a note "To the Reader. This Play being too long to be conveniently Acted, such places as might be least prejudicial to the Plot or Sense, are left out upon the Stage: but that we may no way wrong the incomparable Author, are here inserted according to the Original Copy with this Mark ".".[59]

---

[56] We know that Katherine Corey took the vital role of Sempronia only because Pepys and others tell us so.

[57] The 1661 quarto makes no mention of current performance, although the play was in the Red Bull repertory as of August 1660 and was performed by the King's Company on 3 December 1660. See *The London Stage*, Part 1, pp. 12 and 22.

[58] The names of the performers of four minor parts are omitted.

[59] The two "1676" *Hamlet* quartos (Q6 and Q7) offer a convenient and sobering glimpse of some complexities and complications from which we need to take warning. Emma Depledge (2018)

Fourth, *The Dutchess of Malfey: A Tragedy.* "As it is now Acteed [*sic*] at the Dukes Theater" (1678). Neither title page nor prelims names the author, which is unusual for a reprint of a well-known professional playwright. One might have thought that John Webster's name would have some sales value, and the editions of 1623 and 1640 had duly announced "Written by John Webster" on the title page. "The ACTORS Names" are set against fifteen parts. There is no other paratext. Only four performances are recorded with dates in the late seventeenth century: 30 September 1662, 25 November 1668, 31 January 1672, and 13 January 1686. Of fifteen named members of the cast, at least four cannot be confirmed as members of the Duke's Company in 1678. Extant records suggest that this cast could not have been assembled at any time after autumn 1672, yet the list was not updated for publication in 1678. Perhaps the play remained unper-formed in that span, but the unrevised list is not conclusive evidence.

Fifth, Beaumont and Fletcher's *The Scornful Lady.* "As it was acted with great Applause by the late Kings Majesties Servants, at the Black-Fryers ... The Seventh Edition Corrected and Amended ... 1677." This play had long been popular, and it remained exceptionally so: we have record of ten perform-ances in the 1660s. It was premiered circa 1613–16 and published as a singleton in 1616. The seventh edition lists "The Names of the ACTORS," but this is misleading: what is given are the characters' names, not those of the performers. The eighth edition (1691 – not in the English Short Title Catalogue [ESTC] as of February 2022, but available in EEBO) changes the venue formula to "As it is now Acted at the Theatre Royal, by Their Majesties Servants," but makes no other alterations or additions. It even preserves the spelling of "a Sutur" (suitor) in the identification of two characters. No copy of the putative ninth edition is known to ESTC, but "The Tenth Edition" proves highly problematic. Some copies carry no date, but others do. Both states have a prologue, and an epilogue spoken by Will Pinkethman "mounted on an Ass; a long Whig on the Ass's Head," plus a cast dotted with such names as Wilks, Doggett, Mrs Oldfield, and Cibber. As of May 2022, ESTC R28894 dates the edition "[1695?]," but this is preposterous. The title page reads, "As it is now Acted at the Theatre Royal, by Her Majesty's Company of Comedians," which means that it cannot possibly date from earlier than March 1702, when King William died and Queen Anne succeeded to the throne. Robert Wilks was in and out of London and is not known to have taken any leading roles until 1699. Barton Booth did not perform in London before 1700. The *Biographical Dictionary* reports that Pinkethman

---

has recently made a compelling case (largely from paper and watermark evidence) that Q7 was in fact not published in 1676, but was actually a reprint circa 1683–4 furnished "with a false date and imprint." Her article is a timely reminder that we cannot simply assume the accuracy of bibliographical information found on the title pages of late seventeenth-century plays.

was performing "ass epilogues" from circa August 1702.[60] W. W. Greg unchar-
acteristically fails to realize the significance of "Her Majesty's Company of
Comedians," and says merely that "The BM catalogue queries 1695 as the
date."[61] In fact, the cast as printed in the undated tenth edition correlates almost
perfectly with the cast as advertised at the Queen's Theatre on 11 February 1710.
I note that under citation number T32940, the ESTC dates what appears to be
exactly the same edition "[1710?]."

Obviously, that "tenth" edition has been dated correctly by some modern
scholars but misdated by some fifteen years by others. How much paratext
information should the bibliographer report? It is mostly mechanical, obvious,
and boring – until one little bit turns out to be crucial. The ESTC reportage
understandably tends to be bare-bones, and subsequent editions often repeat
outmoded information for decades. This is all the more reason for scholars to
examine the original paratext now available in EEBO and Eighteenth Century
Collections Online (ECCO) with full texts, rather than assume that ESTC will
suffice. In recent years, ESTC cataloguing has become more rigorously
detailed, though many scholars do not seem to have used the "error" button to
point out needed corrections, easy though that now is to do.

Sixth, Shakespeare's *Othello, the Moor of Venice: A Tragedy* was duly
attributed to William Shakespeare and printed for Bentley and Magnes in
1681. The title page reports, "As it hath been divers times acted at the *Globe*,
and at the *Black-Friers*: And now at the Theater Royal, by His Majesties
Servants." The paratext consists of a page devoted to listing thirty-seven
singleton plays printed for Bentley and Magnes (plus a fifty-play collection of
Beaumont and Fletcher, and six novels), and a Dramatis Personae listing
thirteen named roles and the actor or actress playing each of them. The scene
is specified as "Cyprus." The cast is definitely for a post-1660 King's Company
production of *Othello*, but when? The phrase "And now at the Theater Royal"
seems to imply performance in 1681. We have no record of any performance of
Othello between February 1676 and January 1683, but of course our performance calendar is radically incomplete.[62] Given publication in 1681 and present
tense ("And now") in the venue statement, we might hypothesize that *Othello*

---

[60] Highfill, Burnim, and Langhans (1973–93), 11:322.

[61] Greg (1939–62), 1:476–481 (no. 334).

[62] Of an estimated 14,067 professional performances in London in the period 1660–1700, we have
title and exact date for just 949 (6.7%). From first-run norms and anecdotal evidence about
success, we can infer about 1,502 (another 10.7%) additional performances. We have no
information about 11,616 (82.6%) days. There are huge differences from season to season. In
1667–8, we know 120 of 496 (24%) estimated performances, but in 1669–70 (lacking Pepys's
diary, which ended 1 June 1669), we know only 7 of 328 (2%). In 1678–9, we do not know
a single definite title/date for either company. See Hume (2016).

was in the King's Company's current repertory in 1681. It very likely was, but that would be a risky conclusion.

The London Stage editors constructed company rosters for each season and, given the large number of new plays acted and published with cast names in the 1670s, those rosters usually seem relatively complete. Verifying availability of the performers listed in the cast for *Othello* published in 1681, I find potent evidence that the group specified probably could not have been assembled after the 1674–5 season. Of the performance on 25 January 1675, the *London Stage* editors correctly observe that "The cast in the edition of 1681 may not, of course, be the one for this performance; but all the performers named in it could have performed at this time."[63] Why a cast for a performance closer to publication in 1681 was not printed we can only guess (presuming that there probably was one or more). I note also that when Bentley reprinted *Othello* in 1687 and again in 1695, he retained the title page "Acted ... now" and "His Majesties Servants" (presumably referring in the original instance to Charles II, in the second to James II, and in the third to William) – and the hopelessly dated cast remained unchanged. Not updating casts seems to have been standard operating procedure until well into the second half of the eighteenth century. The rhetoric of title pages can be treacherous, and updating may or may not be carried out in subsequent editions – but in the late seventeenth century, mostly not.[64]

Retrospective

Before turning to a broader overview in which paratext is only one part, I want to summarize briefly what I regard as the crucial takeaway from the technical and bibliographical parts of this Element. First, I should stress the degree to which paratext allows us to recover authorial and audience viewpoints and judgments about a century before the efflorescence of extensive newspaper and magazine reviews and commentary. Prefaces and dedications remain seriously understudied by present-day scholars. Issues such as anonymity, collaboration, use of sources, and the importance of casting to the recreation of seventeenth-century authorial design and performance impact depend, *faute de mieux*, largely on paratext, but it remains erratically and insufficiently utilized. I have not tried to extend my paratext survey through the eighteenth century, but especially in the world of Bell's various reprint series (with illustrations), quite a lot changes – a surprising

---

[63] *The London Stage*, Part 1, p. 227.

[64] In "The Name of Othello is not the Name of *Othello*," Gerald Baker makes some interesting points about this particular play that have broader implications. He inquires, "In an early modern playbook, is the title text or paratext?" (42), pointing out that for performance purposes, "Othello" was the title attached to print usages, whereas "The Moor of Venice" is what we find applied to performances.

amount, considering how much of the eighteenth-century repertory consists of "old" plays.[65] Much remains to be done in these realms. Neither have I attempted systematically to confront the knotty problems posed by falsification of title page data and outright piracy in the late seventeenth century beyond pointing out some instances. But I have encountered a dismaying number of them, and until English plays of the period 1660–1800 find their W. W. Greg, skepticism and caution must be considered the better part of valor. The ESTC is a major blessing, but to trust in it unthinkingly is folly. The flood of footnotes accompanying Appendix B is merely a first step toward cleaning up this part of a bibliographic Augean stable.

Overview: The Big Picture, 1590–1800

By way of conclusion, I would like to offer some comments on how paratext of various sorts helps us understand the ways and directions in which English drama was evolving toward the end of the seventeenth century and beyond. Obviously, I am going enormously outside the chronological boundaries announced in my title ("1660–1700"), but a number of readers of my first draft asked how the mass of detail I have catalogued and analyzed for plays published in the late seventeenth century contributes to our grasp of the larger history of which these four decades are merely one part. This is my response.

In many respects, this "evolution" resists tidy conceptualization or quantification, but I believe that my survey underscores, reinforces, and extends the conclusions offered in Paulina Kewes's important book on "authorship" and "appropriation" in the half century following the Restoration. There was no abrupt change of direction. The quantitative parallels between the 1630s and 1660s outlined earlier in this Element are striking. The long-standing idea of a radical break between 1642 and 1660 is largely false. There are, however, major differences between the larger, cheaper theatres catering to a broader public in the first half of the seventeenth century, and the small, expensive, changeable-scenery theatres constructed after 1660, designed to appeal to what was in the last decades of the century a more elite and wealthier audience.[66] The cheapest admission price after 1660 was $1s$ (= $12d$) in the second gallery; the most expensive was in the boxes at $4s$ per spectator. A penny bought entry for standing room in some of the pre-1642 theatres, and so far as we know, $2d$ could purchase space on a bench. A seat in a well-covered section of the auditorium likely could usually be had for

---

[65] For about 150 pages of analysis of such matters, see Milhous and Hume (2015), chapters 5 and 6.

[66] We are cloudier than we would like as to the audience capacities of pre-1642 public theatres, but Shakespeare's Globe, for example, is generally thought to have been able to accommodate circa 3,000 people at various prices. The new 1660s theatres are believed to have held no more than a seventh or an eighth of that total. The new 1670s theatres probably held no more than about a quarter.

$6d.$[67] Even after inflation is taken into account, theatregoing was enormously more expensive after 1660. Inevitably, the audience became more elite, wealthier, and a lot smaller – though it did not stay that way.

The transition from early seventeenth-century norms to post-1660 norms was unquestionably fostered by changes in the rules governing property rights in plays, already discussed. Before 1642, resistance to publication appears to have been considerable.[68] After 1660, the playwright had an unquestioned right to sell his or her script to a publisher for whatever it would bring. When it went into print, the author's name was usually emblazoned on the title page (82%), a drastic contrast with the 48% of plays before 1642 that were announcedly collaborative (20%) or simply anonymous (28%).

A key to understanding the change in how plays were conceived, viewed, and judged (and probably a significant contributor to it) is Gerard Langbaine's *An Account of the English Dramatick Poets. Or, Some Observations And Remarks On the Lives and Writings, of all those that have Publish'd either Comedies, Tragedies, Tragi-Comedies, Pastorals, Masques, Interludes, Farces, or Opera's in the English Tongue* (1691).[69] For its day, Langbaine's *Account* is a bibliographic marvel. In a world without the academic libraries of the nineteenth-century variety that we take for granted, he managed to buy or consult almost all of the plays ever published in English – nearly a thousand of them. He had read them, and he had managed to familiarize himself with an enormous

---

[67] Evidence of price structures between 1590 and 1642 is sketchier than one would hope. Andrew Gurr's discussion of the subject is as good as any known to me. See Gurr (2009), pp. 12, 116–117, 157–159, and 214. He reports a major difference in capacities and prices between the relatively huge "amphitheatres" (e.g., the Globe) and the much smaller indoor theatres (e.g., Blackfriars). Gurr believes that the amphitheatres had cheap standing room, penny and two-penny galleries, and "lords' rooms where the charge was $6d$." Contrariwise, "In the hall playhouses … the basic admission was $6d.$, and a stool on the stage itself cost a further $6d$. The boxes at the side of the stage cost half-a-crown [$2s$ $6d$]" (214). The rates stand in sharp contrast: 1–$6d$ versus $6d$–$2s$ $6d$.

[68] This is a somewhat dark and contested subject. For discussion, see Milhous and Hume (2015), prologue and chapter 1 (particularly pp. 6–13, 22–30, 43–51, 52–54). I must point out that the long-standing belief that before 1642, companies avoided publication in order to prevent other companies from staging the show ignores the fact that the license often (though not invariably) specifically authorizes only a particular company to perform the text. This raises considerable doubt as to how great was the danger of piracy.

[69] I should not fail to mention at least three other crucial contributors to our knowledge of attribution and performance information concerning late seventeenth-century plays. John Downes's *Roscius Anglicanus* (1708) was long dismissed as the meanderings of an old man in retirement – he had served as prompter for the Duke's, United, and Betterton's companies from the 1660s to 1706. But close examination of every detail has demonstrated that he was in fact strikingly accurate. See the 1987 edition by Milhous and Hume. Two other historian/commentators who have been significantly underutilized are Charles Gildon, who built on Langbaine in *The Lives and Characters of the English Dramatick Poets* (1699), and Giles Jacob, author of *The Poetical Register: or, The Lives and Characters of the English Dramatic Poets* (1719). A great deal of what we know about playwrights and plays comes from these rich and seriously underutilized sources.

number of sources, both plays and nondramatic, many of them existing only in French, Spanish, or Italian. Langbaine searches out and excoriates "plagiaries" with savage fervor. He is usually less fierce when the source is acknowledged. The forty-eight pages he devotes to Dryden acknowledge his virtues and successes but condemn his appropriations pretty harshly. The seven pages on Aphra Behn admit the success of many of her plays (and grant that Behn often improved on her sources) while roundly denouncing her for inadequately acknowledged borrowings.

Langbaine did not just pop up out of nowhere near the end of the century. Others had objected before him, although less systematically. Twenty years earlier, in 1671, in his "Preface" to *An Evening's Love*, Dryden defended his use of his sources. "I am tax'd with stealing all my Playes . . . 'Tis true, that where ever I have lik'd any story in a Romance, Novel, or forreign Play, I have made no difficulty, nor ever shall, to take the foundation of it, to build it up, and to make it proper for the *English* Stage."[70] What we see in bits and pieces and fragments in paratexts and elsewhere between circa 1670 and 1700 is a growing discomfort with unacknowledged appropriation, particularly where earlier English plays are concerned. The difference at its extremes is profound. If plays are merely popular entertainment, concocted by committee for the masses, and perhaps published or perhaps not – then we are in one world. But if a new play is a literary exercise, solo composed by a named playwright who wants his originality and genius admired, then we are in a different world altogether. There is by no means a tidy transition from the one to the other, but there is a decided shift in balance.

What we see in the course of the forty years following the Restoration can be succinctly described in four points. First, there was more professionalization as a new generation of playwrights earning their living emerged in the 1660s and 1670s. Second, a strong trend developed toward solo authorship, with acknowledged collaboration almost vanishing. Third, concern with "literary" merit increased as opposed to merely pulling in paying customers. Restoration drama aimed at a relatively elite and wealthy audience, and many of the playwrights hoped their work would be judged and valued for aesthetic and moral qualities. Concomitantly, fourth, "originality" was increasingly valued, and disclosure of the use of source materials became expected, even demanded. Curiously enough, the evolution that paratext helps us trace through the seventeenth century was halted and in fact actually reversed in the course of the eighteenth.

If Gerard Langbaine had lived another ten years into the start of the eighteenth century, what would he have predicted the future of English drama to be in the coming 100 years? He might quite reasonably have imagined that the trends of the

---

[70] *The Works of John Dryden*, 10:210.

past seventy-odd years would evolve along the lines so clear between 1630 and 1700 of more solo authorship and less collaborative and anonymous work, along with ever-increased demand for "literary" quality and originality – or at least full disclosure of sources, English and foreign, dramatic and nondramatic. This is very far from what happened. For a sweeping and authoritative overview, extending essentially through the whole century, I refer the reader to Paulina Kewes's tour-de-force article, "'[A] Play, Which I Presume to Call *Original*': Appropriation, Creative Genius, and Eighteenth-Century Playwriting."[71] I see no need for an extensive review of her findings (with which I am in strong agreement). Playwriting became radically more commercial and less literary. Increasing stress in the second half of the century on the star system led to scripts designed to show off the principal actors. At the beginning of the century, Thomas Betterton earned "not quite three times as much as his treasurer and over six times as much as his doorkeepers," but in the 1790s, J. P. Kemble earned "four times what his treasurer got and about seventy-five times as much as his doorkeepers."[72]

What a moderately prescient Langbaine might have anticipated in 1700 on the evidence of the previous century might well have included declining regulation of performance (as had already happened for print); expansion in the number of competing theatres, with different managements appealing to different segments of the audience; and some support for an elitist enterprise (in rough parallel to late seventeenth-century developments in Paris).[73] But this was not to be.

I would like to conclude with an adjuration: scholars should neither ignore paratext nor treat it as pro forma mechanical apparatus. I have been grappling with these plays for the past half century, and I have found this granular scrutiny of paratext decidedly illuminating. It brings us closer to the viewpoint of the play-wrights and helps us understand what they were pitching to their audience. And the changing patterns in paratext unquestionably assist us in understanding the broader evolution of the drama whose complex history we are trying to comprehend.[74]

---

[71] Kewes (2001).

[72] On the changing structure of theatre companies and the impact of the star system on salaries, see Milhous (1980), p. 22.

[73] On the radically different system of playwright and actor remuneration as it existed in Paris during the last two decades of the seventeenth century, see Lancaster (1941).

[74] For advice, assistance, suggestions, and corrections of various sorts, I am much indebted to Claire Bowditch, Elaine Hobby, Mary Ann O'Donnell, Diana Solomon, and most particularly Judith Milhous and James E. May. And I am grateful to Heidi C. Craig for generously sharing with me an advance draft of her article "The King's Servants in Printed Paratexts, 1594–1695" (2023). Particular thanks go to Mae Casey and Alex Bainbridge of Pennsylvania State Special Collections for help with illustrations.

Appendix A: Cumulative Statistics by Decade and in Toto

The figures reported here, decade by decade and for the period as a whole, are calculated from the data recorded in each category as reported in Appendix B.[1] The first figure in each column records the number of plays premiered in the decade at issue and published (usually the same year or the next) that *do* contain the specified item of paratext. The figure after the slash (/) records the number of plays in that decade that do *not* contain that item of paratext. So for "Author named" (usually on the title page) for the 68 plays in the 1660s, 56 (82%) name the author and 12 (18%) do not. If the author is named elsewhere (most commonly in signing a dedication), I have included the case as "author named."[2] Percentages are usually rounded to the nearest whole number.

---

[1] The choice of breakdown by decade is not arbitrary. I experimented with other possibilities – for example, I. Beginnings (1660–5). II. King's–Duke's intense competition (1667–82). III. The United Company (1682–94). IV. The actors' rebellion and the resumption of competition (1695–1700). But the resultant figures seemed merely to reinforce things we already knew. A decade-by-decade approach imposes no particular meaning and is interpretively neutral.

[2] In three instances, defective EEBO copies could not be tabulated for title page data (principally attribution, genre, and venue): Bulteel's *Amorous Orontus* (pub. 1665), [Davenant's] *The Rivals* (pub. 1668), and Part 1 of Durfey's *Massaniello* (pub. 1700). In these cases, I have relied on ESTC transcriptions.

Category of paratext	1661–70 68 plays		1671–80 125 plays[3]		1681–90 61 plays		1691–1700 123 plays	
	Yes/No	percentages	Yes/No	percentages	Yes/No	percentages	Yes/No	percentages
Author named	56/12	82%/18%	101/24	81%/19%	57/4	93%/7%	94/29	76%/24%
Subtitle added to title	23/45	34%/66%	59/66	47%/53%	38/23	62%/38%	57/66	46%/54%
Genre designated	55/13	81%/19%	109/16	87%/13%	54/7	89%/11%	116/7	94%/6%
Company/venue	55/13	81%/19%	124/1	99%/1%	61/0	100%/0%	119/4	97%/3%
Licensed for publication	19/49	28%/72%	50/61[4]	40%/48%	11/21	18%/34%	0/ca.35?	0%/100%[5]
Dedication	20/48	29%/71%	74/51	59%/41%	40/21	66%/34%	95/28	77%/23%
Preface or essay	21/47	31%/69%	22/103	18%/82%	16/45	26%/74%	46/77	37%/63%
Characters listed	65/3	96%/4%	123/2	98.4%/1.6%	60/1	98.3%/1.7%	122/1	99%/1%
Connections explained	62/6	91%/9%	100/25	80%/20%	51/10	82%/18%	106/17	86%/14%
described	18/50	26%/74%	49/76	39%/61%	33/28	56%/44%	61/62	49%/51%
Actors' names specified	19/49	28%/72%	79/46	63%/37%	46/15	72%/28%	100/23	81%/19%
Location specified	49/19	72%/28%	103/22	82%/18%	44/17	64%/36%	82/41	67%/33%
Prologue/epilogue	50/18	74%/26%	120/5	96%/4%%	59/2	95%/5%	120/3	97.5%/2.5%

---

[3] This total counts Part 2 of Crowne's *The Destruction of Jerusalem*, published with Part 1 but for which its own prologue and epilogue were supplied.

[4] Because licensing for publication lapsed for about six years in June 1679, its total "Yes plus No" counts for the seventies and eighties (111 of 125 and 32 of 61) differ significantly from other categories. But the percentage calculation reports the proportion of the total output for the decade, not that of the plays that we can estimate *should* have been licensed.

[5] The exact number of plays published before the expiration of the licensing requirement on 3 May 1695 cannot be determined with confidence. But regardless of what the number published may have been, the number licensed was nil.

Category	Yes	No
Author named	308 (82%)	69 (18%)
Subtitle added to title	177 (47%)	200 (53%)
Genre designated	334 (88%)	43 (12%)
Company/venue	359 (95%)	18 (5%)
Licensed for publication[6]	80 (35% est.)	165 (65% est.)
Dedication	229 (61%)	148 (39%)
Preface or essay	105 (28%)	272 (72%)
Characters listed	370 (98%)	7 (2%)
Connections between characters explained	319 (85%)	58 (15%)
Characters described	161 (43%)	216 (57%)
Actors' names specified	244 (65%)	133 (35%)
Location specified	278 (74%)	99 (26%)
Prologue/epilogue	349 (93%)	28 (7%)

Cumulative figures for the 377 plays across the whole forty-year period follow.

---

[6] The eighty licenses are demonstrable fact. The figure of circa 230 plays that appeared during the periods when licensing was in force is my best guess (we do not know the exact publication date for a number of plays), but it should be accurate within a few either way. I am confident that no more than one-third of the plays that *ought* to have been licensed were indeed licensed. Considered against the 377 total number, only about 21% actually did get licensed.

Appendix B: Twelve Varieties of Paratext in New English Printed Plays, 1660–1700

Plays published more than one calendar year after premiere have the publication year **bolded**. Plays not published in the seventeenth century are (for obvious reasons) omitted – for example, Orrery's *The General*, which was performed in 1664 and survived in manuscript, but was not published until 1937. Playwrights' names have usually been normalized (e.g., "Southerne" rather than "Southern"). The second column reports the principal title. If it is followed by the symbol ⁑, then there is also a subtitle (usually omitted here). If substantial indebtedness to an earlier play is clearly indicated in the first quarto, that source is identified in the first column, either in parentheses or a footnote (e.g., "adapt. Shakespeare"). If the indebtedness now known is *not* made clear in the prelims, then it is explained in [brackets] or a footnote. If genre is specified on the title page it is reported; if not, an asterisk (*) follows the title. A dagger (†) indicates the presence on the title page of the company and/or theatre as the venue; conversely, an inverted dagger (⊬) indicates *absence* of such information (which is rare).[1] Abbreviations employed in the last column are: Lic = Licence to publish (normally on the title page); Ded = Dedication; Pref = Preface; Loc = location of action specified; P/Ep = prologue and epilogue (P by itself means "prologue only"). [SR] (in brackets) means that the work was entered in the Stationers' Register by the publisher (obviously *not* a part of the paratext).

---

[1] Only seventeen instances among 377 plays, with just two after the 1660s – Ravenscroft's *Titus Andronicus* (published in 1687, more than five years after its premiere) and Part 3 of Durfey's *Don Quixote* (published in 1696).

Plays published between 1661 and 1669

Playwright	Title (and genre if stated)	Publication year	List of characters	Connections explained	Characters described	Names of actors given	Other paratext
		Plays premiered in 1661					
Abraham Cowley	Cutter of Coleman-Street. A Comedy†	1663	Yes	Yes	Yes	No	Pref; Loc; P/Ep[2]
Sir William Davenant	The Siege of Rhodes [two parts published together]*†[3]	1663	Yes	Yes	No	No	Ded; Loc; P/Ep[4]
		Plays premiered in 1662					
Sir William Davenant [adapt. Shakespeare]	The Law against Lovers*†[5]	1673 Works	Yes	Yes	No	No	Loc
Sir Robert Howard	The Committee. A Comedy†	1665 (coll.)[6]	Yes	A few	No	No	Lic; Loc; P/Ep; [SR]
Sir Robert Howard	The Surprisal. A Comedy†	1665 (coll.)	Yes	Yes	No	No	Lic; Loc; P/Ep; [SR]
Sir William Killigrew	Selindra. A Tragi-comedy‡	1665	Yes	Yes	No	No	Lic; Loc[7] [SR]
Thomas Porter	The Villain. A Tragedy‡	1663	Yes	Yes	No	No	Loc; P;[8] [SR]

2 Twelve lines "Added at Court" are appended to the prologue and an "Epilogue At Court" is added at the end of the play.

3 Original versions performed privately under the Cromwell regime and published in 1656 and 1659. The Duke's Company opened the Lincoln's Inn Fields theatre with them in June 1661.

4 Part 1 has in place of a prologue "The Scene before the First Entry," followed by some "Instrumental Musick." A "Chorus of Souldiers" serves as an epilogue. Part 2 has prologue and epilogue.

5 Unacknowledged adaptation of Shakespeare's Measure for Measure.

6 Howard published his Four New Plays in 1665, comprising The Surprisal, The Committee, The Indian-Queen, and The Vestal-Virgin. The volume is prefaced by a multipage disquisition addressed "To the Reader." The general title page and two of the individual title pages (those for The Surprisal and The Committee) carry an imprimatur by Roger L'Estrange and the date of March 7, 1664/5. The paratext for each play is identical: P/Ep, and Dramatis Personae lists without actors' names. Performance auspices were announced on the general title page ("As they were Acted by His MAJESTIES Servants at the Theatre-Royal"), but not on the title pages of the four plays.

7 A manuscript prologue and epilogue (both quite short) were found by Johnston and Vander Motten and published in Modern Philology in 1979. They are reprinted by Danchin (1981–8), Part I, 1:119–120.

8 An epilogue by Davenant was printed in volume 1 of his 1673 Works and published by Danchin (1981–8), Part I, 1:30–31.

(cont.)

Playwright	Title (and genre if stated)	Publication year	List of characters	Connections of characters explained	Characters described	Names of actors given	Other paratext
		Plays premiered in 1663					
Anon. [Sir William Killigrew][9]	Pandora. A Comedy*‡	1664	Yes	Yes	No	No	Lic; Loc; P/Ep;[10] [SR]
Anon. [Sir Robert Stapylton][11]	The Step-Mother. A Tragi-Comedy†	1664	Yes	Yes	No	Yes	Lic; Stationer to Reader; Loc; P/Ep[12]
Anon. [John Wilson][13]	The Cheats. A Comedy‡	1664	Yes	Yes	No	No	Lic; Author to Reader; Loc; P/Ep;[14] [SR]
"Written by the Lord Viscount Favvlkland"[15]	The Mariage Night*‡	1664	Yes	Yes	No	No	Lic;[16] Loc
Sir William Davenant	The Play-house to be Let*‡	1673 (Coll.)	No	No	No	No	[Loc];[17] P/Ep
John Dryden	The Wild Gallant. A Comedy†	1669	Yes	Yes	A bit	No	Pref; Loc; P/Ep;[18] [SR]

---

9   Published anonymously in the singleton of 1664 but included in Killigrew's *Three New Plays* in 1665. Downes (1987, 59) states that it was performed at Lincoln's Inn Fields. Date unknown.

10 Killigrew's *Three Plays* (1665) reprints *Pandora* and contains complementary poems by Edmund Waller and Lodowick Carlisle (among others) specifically concerning that play but that do not appear in the 1664 quarto.

11 Published anonymously and treated that way by early authorities, but the prologue explicitly states that the playwright was the author of *The Slighted Maid*, the dedication of which Stapylton signed. Confirmation appeared in a publisher's advertisement in *The Newes* (12 May 1664), which states that *The Step-Mother* was "Acted with great Applause" at Lincoln's Inn Fields and was "Written by Sir Robert Stapylton."

12 Also prologue and epilogue to the king at Whitehall.

13 On attribution and the play's difficulties with censorship, see Nahm's edition of John Wilson's *The Cheats* (1935).

14 Also "Another [prologue] Intended, upon the revival of the Play, but not spoken."

15 The *London Stage* editors question whether "Viscount Falkland" refers to Henry Cary (4th Viscount) or Lucius Cary (2nd Viscount), Part 1 (1965), p. 71.

16 Licensed 16 October 1663, license coming abnormally at the end of the prelims.

17 The location of the action is not specified, but it is of course the Lincoln's Inn Fields playhouse, where the play was being performed.

18 Prints both original 1663 prologue and epilogue and those for a revival probably in 1667.

		Year				Paratext
Richard Flecknoe	*Love's Kingdom. A Pastoral Trage-Comedy*[19]	1664	Yes	A bit	No	Lic; Ded; "To the noble Readers"; Loc; P[20]
James Howard	*The English Mounsieur: A Comedy*†	**1674**	Yes	Some	No	Loc
Thomas Porter	*The Carnival. A Comedy*†	1664	Yes	No	No	Loc
Robert Stapylton[21]	*The Slighted Maid. A Comedy*†	1663	Yes	Yes	Yes	Ded; Loc; P/Ep[22]
Sir Samuel Tuke[23]	*The Adventures of Five Hours. A Tragi-Comedy*‡	1663	Yes	No	No	Lic; Ded; Loc; P/Ep;[24]

Plays premiered in 1664[25]

Anon. [George Villiers Second Duke of Buckingham][26]	*The Chances* [adapted from Fletcher]. *A Comedy*†	1682	No	No	No	P/Ep
Anon. [Davenant] [adapting Shakespeare][27]	*Macbeth. A Tragedy*†	1674	Yes	No	Some	Argument

---

19 Flecknoe's title page reads, "Not as it was Acted at the Theatre near *Lincolns-Inn*, but as it was written and since corrected."

20 "A Short Discourse of the English Stage" follows the text of the play, as do the words for two songs.

21 Stapylton signed the dedication.   22 Also prologue and epilogue "to the King."

23 Tuke signed the dedication.   24 Also prologue and epilogue at court.

25 Sir William Killigrew's *Ormasdes, or Love and Friendship* (a tragicomedy) is a good example of a borderline case. It was licensed for publication on 23 August 1664 and published in 1665 with no paratext indicating performance. A holograph prologue and epilogue for the play were written into Killigrew's personal copy of a collection published in 1666. Danchin (1981–8) prints them (Part 1, 1:171–172) and says, "The play is likely to have been performed some time in the season preceding its licensing." J. P. Vander Motten (1980) is dubious: "Whether the play was ever performed, must remain a moot point" (159). In the absence of definite proof of performance, I have excluded it from my statistics.

26 The title page ascription says "Corrected and Altered by a Person of Honour." Published eighteen years after the premiere (very possibly unauthorized) and without paratext other than prologue and epilogue.

27 This is a confusing case. The 1674 edition carries no authorial ascription, but the title page does say, "With all the Alterations, Amendments, Additions, and new songs. *As it's now Acted at the Dukes Theatre.*" This appears to have been the text staged by the Duke's Company in November 1664 and published as "Printed for *P. Chetwin*, and are to be Sold by most Booksellers, 1674." Curiously enough, a year earlier, William Cademan had published *Macbeth: A Tragedy. Acted At the Dukes-Theatre*, with the same Duke's Company cast, though the text is that of the First Folio with some very minor additions. See Spencer (1963), pp. 152–174. Neither edition ever mentions either Shakespeare's name or Davenant's.

Playwright	Title (and genre if stated)	Publication year	List of characters given	Connections explained	Characters described	Names of actors given	Other paratext
Anon. [Sir William Davenant] [adaptation]²⁸	The Rivals. A Comedy†	1668	Yes	Yes	No	Yes	Lic; Loc [implicit]; [SR]
Anon.²⁹	Pompey the Great. A Tragedy. (Translated from Corneille)†	1664	Yes	Yes	No	No	P/Ep;³⁰ [SR]
Anon. "Written by a Person of Quality" [George Digby?]	Elvira.³¹ A Comedy*‡	1667	Yes	Yes	No	No	[Lic];³² Loc
Anon.³³ [Richard Rhodes]	Flora's Vagaries. A Comedy†	1670	Yes	Yes	No	Several	Lic
John Bulteel [trans. Corneille]	Amorous Orontus. A Comedy[‡]	1665	Yes	No	No	No	None;³⁴ [SR]

28 Adaptation of Fletcher and Shakespeare's *The Two Noble Kinsmen* (published in 1634). The EEBO copy lacks prelims, but the 1668 edition mentions neither the source nor Davenant. The ESTC reports performance by the Duke's company and licensing for publication on 19 September 1668. Attributed to Davenant by both Langbaine (1691), p. 547, and Downes (1987), p. 55. It was not included in Herringman's 1673 folio *Works* for reasons unknown to me.

29 "Translated out of French by Certain Persons of Honour." This was a group enterprise. Katherine Philips wrote on 10 January 1662/3 to "Poliarchus" (Sir Charles Cotterell) that "I have laid out several ways to get a Copy, but cannot yet procure one, except only of the first Act that was done by Mr. Waller. Sir Edward Filmore [Sir Edward Filmer] did one, Sir Charles Sedley another, and my Lord Buckhurst [i.e., the sixth Earl of Dorset to be] another; but who the fifth I cannot learn, pray inform your self as soon as you can, and let me know it" (Philips [1705], Letter 23, pp. 112–113).

30 The 1664 edition actually prints three epilogues, one used in the theatre, one "To the King at Saint *James*'s," and the other "To the Duchess at Saint *James*'s."

31 *Elvira* is a troublesome case. It has been widely assumed to be by George Digby, Earl of Bristol, a plausible attribution.

32 Nicoll (1:403) and *The London Stage* (Part 1, p. 95) both report an imprimatur of 15 May 1667, but it is lacking in one of the two EEBO copies. I am grateful to Claire Bowditch for pointing out to me the existence of the second EEBO copy, which carries a portrait of Digby opposite the title page.

33 Langbaine (1691), p. 532, says "ascribed to Mr. *Rhodes*." Both *The London Stage* (Part 1, p. 72) and all three editions of the *Annals of English Drama 975–1700* (by Harbage, Schoenbaum, and Wagonheim) place the premiere in November 1663, but this is demonstrably wrong. See Bond (1986). The correct date is almost certainly March or possibly April 1664.

34 This is a verse translation of Corneille's *L'amour à la mode.* The EEBO copy (Bodleian) lacks prelims, but neither the *London Stage* nor other authorities report paratextual material. The 1675 reprint describes the play as "'A Comedie, In Heroick Verse, As it was Acted." Performance by the King's Company at Bridges Street during the 1663–4 season seems probable.

John Dryden[35]	The Rival Ladies. A Tragi-Comedy†	1664	Yes	No	No	Ded; P;[36] Loc; [SR]
George Etherege[37]	The Comical Revenge*†	1664	Ye s	Some	No[38]	Lic; Ded; P/Ep;[39] [SR]
Edward Howard	The Usurper. A Tragedy†	**1668**	Yes	A bit	No	Lic; Epistle; Loc; P/Ep; [SR]
Sir Robert Howard	The Vestal-Virgin.* A Tragedy [but with alternative comic ending]†	1665 (coll.)	Yes	Some	No	Loc; P/Ep; see note;[40] [SR]
Sir Robert Howard [& Dryden?]	The Indian-Queen.[41] A Tragedy†	1665 (coll.)	Yes	No	No	P/Ep (see note 86); [SR]
Sir William Killigrew	The Seege of Urbin. A Tragy-Comedy[42] ‡	1666 (coll.)	Some	No	No	Author to Reader; Loc; P/Ep[43]
John Lacy	The Old Troop. A Comedy**†	1672	A bit	No	No	Ded; Epistle to Reader; P/Ep
Roger Boyle, Earl of Orrery	The History of Henry the Fifth†	**1668**	Yes	No	Yes	Loc;[44] [SR]

35 Not attributed on the title page, but Dryden signed the dedication.

36 Followed by "A second Prologue."

37 Etherege is not credited on the title page, but he signed the dedication.

38 Downes gives us the cast, Roscius Anglicanus, p. 56.

39 Two short epilogues are printed without explanation.

40 Howard supplied both a tragic version and an alternative happy-ending version, with an appropriate epilogue for each.

41 Published in Howard's Four New Plays (1665), not as a singleton. Dryden's involvement was apparently minimal. See Spielman (2008).

42 Published in Killigrew's Four New Plays (1666). Annals of English Drama (3rd edition, pp. 168–169) says "Unacted?" The London Stage (Part 1, p. 82) notes the existence of a King's Company cast in a holograph copy at Oxford. On revisions and additions in Sir William Killigrew's personal copy of Four New Plays, see Vander Motten and Johnston (1983). The cast may be hypothetical and the revisions unused, but on balance professional performance seems likely.

43 Four commendatory poems are included in the prelims.

44 Stated scene by scene, not on the Dramatis Personae page.

Playwright	Title (and genre if stated)	Publication year	List of characters explained	Connections explained	Characters described	Names of actors given	Other paratext
		Plays premiered in 1665					
John Dryden	The Indian Emperour[45] **‡	**1667**	Yes	Yes	No	No	Ded; Loc; P/Ep;[46] [SR]
James Howard	All Mistaken. A Comedy *†	**1672**	Yes	Yes	A bit	No	Loc[47]
Roger Boyle, Earl of Orrery	The Tragedy of Mustapha†	**1668**	Yes	Yes	No	Yes	Loc;[48] [SR]
	Theatres were closed on account of plague in 1666. Plays premiered in 1667						
Anon. [William Cavendish, Duke of Newcastle and Dryden][49]	Sir Martin Mar-all. A Comedy*†	1668	Yes	Some	No	No	Loc; P/Ep; [SR]
Anon. [John Carel?][50]	The English Princess. A Tragedy*‡	1667	Yes	Some	No	No	Lic; Loc; P/Ep; [SR]
Davenant and Dryden (adapting Shakespeare)[51]	The Tempest. A Comedy*†	**1670**	Yes	Some	Some	No	Pref signed by Dryden; P/Ep; [SR]

---

45 Lack of title page announcement of performance auspices and/or theatre is exceedingly rare, especially in a book published by Herringman. The omission was almost certainly unintentional. We know the cast from Downes (1987), p. 26.

46 Also contains "A Defence of an Essay of Dramatique Poesie," written in "Answer" to Sir Robert Howard, running to some 8,000 words, plus an explanation of the "Connexion of the Indian Emperour, to the Indian Queen."

47 The London Stage, Part 1, p. 118, places the play in 1667 when Pepys attended it. But he says, "I do not remember that I have seen it" (20 September). On the date, see Hume (1972). There is potent evidence for premiere in spring 1665.

48 Stated scene by scene, not on the Dramatis Personae page.

49 The quarto of 1668 contains no hint of authorship. Pepys attended on 16 August 1667 and called it "a play made by my Lord Duke of Newcastle, but as everybody says corrected by Dryden." It was not published with Dryden's name attached until 1691.

50 Langbaine (1691), p. 530, says, "Ascribed to Mr. John Carel."

51 No authorial credit is given on the title page, but Dryden's 1670 preface says, "It was originally Shakespear's" and explains his collaboration with Davenant.

John Dryden	*Secret-Love***†	1668	Yes	Some	No	Yes	Pref; Loc; P/Ep;[52] [SR]
John Lacy [adapting Shakespeare]	*Sauny the Scot: or the Taming of the Shrew*. A Comedy*†	1698	Yes	A few	No	Yes[53]	None
William Cavendish, Duke of Newcastle [and collaborator?]	*The Humorous Lovers*. A Comedy†	1677	Yes	Yes	A bit	No	Lic; Loc[54]
Roger Boyle, Earl of Orrery	*The Black Prince*, published with *Tryphon* as "Two New Tragedies"†	1669	Yes	No	No	Yes	P/Ep; location implicit; [SR]
Thomas St Serfe	*Tarugo's Wiles*. A Comedy*†	1668	Yes	A bit	No	No	Ded; P/Ep[55]
Plays premiered in 1668							
Sir William Davenant [trans. Scarron]	*The Man's the Master*. A Comedy‡	1669	Yes	Yes	No	No	Loc; P/Ep; [SR]
Sir John Denham completing K. Philips[56]	*Horace*. A Tragedy‡	1669	Yes	Yes	No	No	Loc
John Dryden	*An Evening's Love***†	1671	Yes	Yes	Yes	Yes	Ded; Pref;[57] Loc; P/Ep; [SR]
George Etherege	*She wou'd if she cou'd*. A Comedy†	1668	Yes	A few	No	No[58]	None; [SR]

---

52 Triple prologue, two epilogues.

53 The cast is for a Patent Company revival circa 1698.

54 Covent Garden is specified in I.i.

55 Location is "A Coffee-House."

56 A translation of Pierre Corneille's *Horace* (1640), left incomplete by Katherine Phillips but published posthumously in her *Poems* (1667). Completed by Sir John Denham, who added the fifth act published in the second edition of Phillips' *Poems* in 1669. A prologue (by John Crowne) spoken at court in February 1668 was published in the *Covent Garden Drollery* (1672).

57 Dryden's preface is a meaty essay of some 4,500 words – one of the most important statements on comedy from the late seventeenth century.

58 The cast is given by Downes (1987), p. 63.

(cont.)

Playwright	Title (and genre if stated)	Publication year	List of characters	Connections explained	Characters described	Names of actors given	Other paratext
Sir Robert Howard[59]	The Great Favourite**†	1668	Yes	Yes	No	No	To the Reader; Loc; P/Ep; [SR]
Roger Boyle, Earl of Orrery	Tryphon, second title in Two New Tragedies†	1669	Yes	Some	No	No	Loc;[60] P/Ep; [SR]
Sir Charles Sedley	The Mulberry-Garden. A Comedy†	1668	Yes	A few	No	No	Ded; P/Ep
Thomas Shadwell	The Sullen Lovers. A Comedy*†	1668	Yes	A few	Yes	No	Ded; Pref; Loc; P/Ep; [SR]
Plays premiered in 1669							
Anon. [adapting Fletcher][61]	The Island Princess. A Comedy*†	1669	Yes	No	No	Yes	Lic; P/Ep[62]
Roger Boyle, Earl of Orrery	Mr. Anthony. A Comedy†	1690	Yes	Yes	No	Yes	Lic;[63] P/Ep
Roger Boyle, Earl of Orrery	Guzman. A Comedy†	1693	Yes	Yes	A bit	No	Ded;[64] Loc; [SR]

59 Howard's "To the Reader" says that the company showed him an old MS play that would not do, but inspired him to write a play on its subject. Alfred Harbage has argued persuasively that The Great Favourite, Or; The Duke of Lerma is, in fact, merely an adaptation of John Ford's (?) The Spanish Duke of Lerma (1629 or later; entered in the Stationers' Register in 1653; never published; lost). See Harbage (1940), pp. 297–304.

60 Location is specified scene by scene, not in the Dramatis Personae.

61 Fletcher is not identified as the source, but the title page does say: "As it is Acted at the Theatre Royal . . . With the Alterations and New Additional Scenes."

62 The prologue was borrowed without acknowledgment from Fletcher's The Noble Gentleman (1606? Rev. 1625).

63 Licensed 27 August 1689 at the time of publication, though the cast is for performance in 1669. No revival is known.

64 The earl died in 1679. The dedication was supplied by Nahum Tate.

Mrs. F. Boothby	Marcelia. A Tragi-comedy*†	1670	Yes	A bit	No	Lic; Ded; Loc; P/Ep
John Dryden	Tyrannick Love. A Tragedy*†	1670	Yes	No	Yes	Ded; Pref; Loc; P/Ep; [SR]
John Lacy	The Dumb Lady**†	1672	Yes	No	No	Ded; Epistle to Reader; P/Ep
Thomas Shadwell	The Royal Shepherdess. A Tragi-Comedy†	1669	Yes	A bit	No	To the Reader; Loc; P/Ep; [SR]

Plays published between 1670 and 1679

Playwright	Title (and genre if stated)	Publication year	List of characters	Connections explained	Characters described	Names of actors given	Other paratext
		Plays premiered in 1670[65]					
Anon. [John Caryll? trans. Molière][66]	Sir Salomon. A Comedy*†	1671	Yes	Yes	No	No	Loc; P/Ep; [SR]
Aphra Behn	The Forced Marriage. A Tragi-Comedy*†	1671	Yes	Yes	No	Yes	Loc; P/Ep
John Dryden	The Conquest of Granada I & II*† [two parts]	1672	Yes	Yes	No	Yes	Ded; Pref;[67] Loc; P/Ep; P/Ep (both parts); [SR]
E. H. [Edward Howard]	The Womens Conquest. A Tragi-Comedy†	1671	Yes	Yes	A bit	Yes	Preface; Loc; P/Ep;[68] [SR]
William Joyner	The Roman Empress. A Tragedy†	1671	Yes	Yes	No	Yes	Ded; Pref; Loc; [SR]
Matthew Medbourne (trans. Molière)	Tartuffe. A Comedy*†	1670	No	No	No	No	Ded; P/Ep;[69] [SR]
Thomas Shadwell	The Humorists. A Comedy†	1671	Yes	Yes	Yes	No	Ded; Preface; Loc; P/Ep

[65] I have excluded Thomas Betterton's The Amorous Widow – a play of some importance – from my paratext statistics because it is a unique and peculiar case. The play was a translation/adaptation concoction drawn from Thomas Corneille's Le Baron d'Albikrac and Molière's George Dandin. Downes (1987) records it with a partial cast among a group of plays performed at Lincoln's Inn Fields in the latter part of the 1660s (p. 65). It was not published until 1706 because Betterton notoriously resisted publication of any of his work (all of it translation/adaptation). On this case, see Milhous (1974).

[66] Attributed to Caryll by Langbaine (1691), p. 547, from hearsay ("as I have heard"). Acknowledged in the epilogue as translation from Molière. This is an Englished version of L'Ecole des Femmes.

[67] The preface is a substantial essay, "Of Heroique Playes," running to ten pages of print.

[68] Howard's preface is a meaty critical essay of twenty-five pages; there are actually three linked prologues.

[69] The EEBO copy is defective at the start of the text. For complete and annotated texts, see Danchin (1981–8), Part I, 2:367–369.

Plays premiered in 1671

Author	Title						
Anon. [George Villiers, Second Duke of Buckingham][70]	The Rehearsal* †	1672	Yes	No	No	No	Loc; P/Ep; [SR]
Anon. [Edward Howard][71]	The Six days Adventure. A Comedy*†	1671	Yes	No	No	Yes	Pref; Loc; P/Ep[72]
Aphra Behn	The Amorous Prince. A Comedy*†	1671	Yes	Yes	A bit	No	Loc; P/Ep
John Corye	The Generous Enemies. A Comedy*†	1672	Yes	Yes	A bit	Yes	Lic; Loc; P/Ep
John Crowne	Juliana or the Princess of Poland. A Tragi-comedy*†	1671	Yes	Yes	A bit	Yes	Lic; Ded; Loc; P/Ep
John Crowne	The History of Charles the Eighth of France**†	1672	Yes	Yes	A bit	Yes	Ded; Loc; P/Ep [SR]
John Dryden	Marriage A-la-Mode. A Comedy†[73]	1673	Yes	Yes	No	Yes	Ded; Loc; P/Ep; [SR]
Edward Revet[74]	The Town-Shifts. A Comedy*†	1671	Yes	No	No	Yes	Lic; Ded; P/Ep
Elkanah Settle	Cambyses King of Persia. A Tragedy†	1671	Yes	Yes	Some	Yes	Lic; Ded; Loc; P/Ep; Postscript
William Wycherley	Love in a Wood. A Comedy*†	1672	Yes	Yes	Yes	Yes	Ded; Loc; P/Ep; [SR]

[70] Published without attribution, very possibly without the Duke's permission.

[71] Attributed by Langbaine (1691), p. 274.

[72] Plus eight pages of commendatory poems by Aphra Behn and others.

[73] Probably premiered by late November 1671. See Hume (1973).

[74] No attribution on title page, but Revet signed the dedication. The setting is implicitly London.

(cont.)

Playwright	Title (and genre if stated)	Publication year	List of characters	Connections explained	Characters described	Names of actors given	Other paratext
		Plays premiered in 1672					
Anon. [Joseph Arrowsmith][75]	The Reformation. A Comedy†	1673	Yes	Yes	A bit	Yes	Loc; P/Ep
Anon. [Henry Neville Payne][76]	The Fatal Jealousy. A Tragedy†	1673	Yes	Yes	No	Yes	Lic; P/Ep
Anon. [Henry Neville Payne][77]	The Morning Ramble. A Comedy*†	1673	Yes	No	No	Yes	Lic; Loc;[78] P/Ep
John Dryden	The Assignation**†	1673	Yes	Yes	No	Yes	Ded; Loc; P/Ep; [SR]
Edward Ravenscroft	The Citizen Turn'd Gentleman. A Comedy†	1672	Yes	Yes	No	Yes	Lic; Ded; Loc; P/Ep[79]
Thomas Shadwell	Epsom-Wells. A Comedy†	1673	Yes	Yes	Yes	No[80]	Lic; Ded; P/Ep;[81] [SR]
Thomas Shadwell (trans. Molière's L'Avare)	The Miser.[82] A Comedy†	1672	Yes	Yes	No	No	Ded; Note to the "Reader"; P/Ep;
Thomas Shipman	Henry the Third of France. A Tragedy**†	1678	Yes	Some	No	No	Lic; Ded; Loc;[83] P/Ep[84]
William Wycherley	The Gentleman Dancing-Master. A Comedy†	1673	Yes	Yes	Yes	No	Loc; P/Ep; [SR]

75 "This Play is ascribed to Mr. Arrowsmith," according to Langbaine (1691), p. 546.
76 Langbaine (1691), p. 531, says "ascribed by some to Mr. Pane."
77 Langbaine (1691), p. 541, says, "This Play is said to be written by One Mr. Pane."
78 The location is implicitly London ("The Scene Hide-Park," p. 56).
79 Prologue spoken at the Middle Temple appended at the end.
80 But the cast is known from Downes (1987), p. 70.
81 "Prologue to the King and Queen, spoken at Whitehall" added.
82 There is no Dramatis Personae page in one EEBO copy, but another EEBO 1672 copy does have one, printed by Summers in The Complete Works of Thomas Shadwell, 2:19.
83 Exceptionally specific and detailed: "The Scene, Blois, remov'd at the Fourth Act to the Camp at St. Clou, before Paris."
84 Prelims also include an address "To Roger L'Estrange" (the licencer) and a poetic epistle to James, Duke of Monmouth.

Plays premiered in 1673

Anon. [Thomas Duffett?][85]	*The Empress of Morocco. A Farce*†	1674	Yes	Yes	A bit	Yes	Loc implicit; P/Ep
Anon. [Samuel Pordage?][86]	*Herod and Mariamne. A Tragedy*†	1674	Yes	Yes	No	Yes	Ded;[87] Loc; P/Ep; [SR]
Aphra Behn	*The Dutch Lover. A Comedy*†	1673	Yes	Yes	No	No	Pref;[88] Loc; Ep
John Dryden	*Amboyna. A Tragedy**†	1673	Yes	Yes	No	Yes	Ded; Loc; P/Ep; [SR]
Thomas Duffett	*The Spanish Rogue**†	1674	Yes	No	No	Yes	Ded; P/Ep
Edward Ravenscroft	*The Careless Lovers. A Comedy*†	1673	Yes	Some	No	Yes	Epistle; Loc; P/Ep
Elkanah Settle	*The Empress of Morocco. A Tragedy. With Sculptures*†	1673	Yes	A bit	No	Yes	Ded; [Loc]; P/Ep[89]

Plays premiered in 1674

Anon.[90] [Henry Neville Payne]	*The Siege of Constantin-ople. A Tragedy*†	1675	Yes	Some	No	No	P; Loc; [SR]
Anon.[91]	*The Mistaken Husband. A Comedie*†	1675	Yes	Yes	A bit	No	P/Ep

[85] Published anonymously. Langbaine (1691), p. 530, lists the title among the "Unknown Authors" group, saying, "Said to be writ by *Thomas Duffet*." No attribution issue is raised in *Three Burlesque Plays of Thomas Duffett*, ed. Di Lorenzo. Langbaine's attribution may well be true, though *The Mock-Tempest* (pub. 1674) and *Psyche Debauch'd* (pub. 1678) are very different kinds of travesty. A plausible attribution, but not proven, must be the verdict on present evidence.

[86] Attributed without explanation by Langbaine (1691), p. 406, who says the play was given to Elkanah Settle.

[87] Dedication signed by Elkanah Settle, who saw the play to the stage.

[88] Addressed to the "Good, Sweet, Honey, Sugar-candied Reader," reporting prejudice against a woman playwright and mentioning that "The Prologue is by misfortune lost."

[89] Location is implicit in the title. The quarto contains six full-page illustrations, showing the exterior of the Dorset Garden theatre in a frontispiece and five depictions of stage situations. The prelims also include two prologues spoken "at Court," one written by the Earl of Mulgrave, the other by the Earl of Rochester.

[90] Published anonymously. Listed under "Unknown Authors" by Langbaine (1691), p. 549; Gildon [1699], p. 328; Jacob (1719), p. 168, and other early eighteenth-century sources, but in fact attributed bluntly by Downes, who as company prompter ought to have known: "Wrote by Mr. *Nevill Pain*" (p. 75).

[91] The prelims contain a note from "The Bookseller to the Reader" stating that the play had been left with Dryden twelve years earlier by someone he did not know who never reclaimed his work. Dryden reportedly found it good, added a scene, and gave it to the King's Company.

(cont.)

Playwright	Title (and genre if stated)	Publication year	List of characters	Connections explained	Characters described	Names of actors given	Other paratext
Anon. [Updated by Thomas Shadwell][92]	The Tempest [semi-opera version]. A Comedy*†	1674	Yes	Some	No	No	See note[93]
Anon. ("Written By a Person of Honour")[94]	The Amorous Old-woman. A Comedy*†	1674	Yes	Yes	No	Yes	Loc; P/Ep[95]
J. C. [John Crowne][96] (trans. Racine)	Andromache. A Tragedy†	1675	Yes	Yes	No	No	Epistle to the Reader; Loc; P
J.D. [John Dover?]	The Mall. A Comedy*†	1674	Yes	Yes	A bit	No	Ded; Loc; P/Ep
Thomas Duffett	The Mock-Tempest*††	1675	Yes	Some	No	No	Loc; P/Ep
Nathaniel Lee	The Tragedy of Nero†	1675	Yes	Yes	No	Yes	Ded; Loc implicit; P/Ep
William Cavendish, Duke of Newcastle [with Shadwell?]	The Triumphant Widow. A Comedy*†	1677	Yes	Some	A bit	No	Lic; no P; two short Epilogues
P.P. [Pierre Perin][97]	Ariadne, or The Marriage of Bacchus. An Opera[98]*†	1673/4	Yes	Mostly not	No	No	Ded; To the Reader; Loc; P
Elkanah Settle[99]	Love and Revenge. A Tragedy†	1675	Yes	Yes	No	Yes	Ded; P/Ep

92 According to John Downes, in 1673[/4], the Dryden–Davenant revamping of Shakespeare's The Tempest (1667, pub. 1670) was 'made into an Opera by Mr. Shadwell" (pp. 73–74).

93 The preface by Dryden and the prologue and epilogue are taken verbatim from the 1670 edition.

94 Langbaine (1691), p. 526, put the play under "Unknown Authors," but says, "I have been told this Play was writ by Tho. Duffet," though the descriptor applies poorly to him. Gildon removed the sentence in his 1699 revision of Langbaine (1691), p. 156.

95 The prelims include a second prologue, intended but not spoken.

96 Attributed to John Crowne by Langbaine (1691), p. 90.

97 "First Compos'd by Mounsieur P.P. Now put into Musick by Monseiur Grabut."

98 Published simultaneously in French. The statement about venue/auspices is unique: "Acted by the Royall Academy of Musick, at the Theatre-Royal in Covent-Garden." The opera was performed in the recently opened Drury Lane theatre by a newly constituted "Academy of Music" that did not thrive. On this venture, see Danchin (1981–8).

99 Adapting William Hemming's The Fatal Contract (1638–9? Pub. 1653). See Langbaine (1691), p. 442.

Anon.	*Piso's Conspiracy. A Tragedy*†[100]	1676	Yes	Yes	No	No	Loc; P/Ep
Anon.	*The Woman turn'd Bully. A Comedy*†	1675	Yes	Yes	Yes	No	Lic; Loc; P/Ep; [SR]
P. B. [Peter Belon (?)][101]	*The Mock-Duellist. A Comedy**†	1675	Yes	Yes	A bit	No	Lic; Ded; Loc; P/Ep[102]
John Dryden	*Aureng-Zebe. A Tragedy*†	1676	Yes	A few	No	Yes	Lic;[103] Ded; Loc; P/Ep [SR]
Thomas Duffett	*Psyche Debauch'd. A Comedy*†	1678	Yes	Some	No	Yes	P/Ep
Sir Francis Fane, *Junior*	*Love in the Dark. A Comedy**†	1675[104]	Yes	A few	A few	Yes	Ded; Loc;[105] P/Ep; [SR]
Nathaniel Lee	*Sophonisba.*[106] *A Tragedy*†	1676	Yes	Some	Some	Yes	Ded; Loc
Thomas Otway	*Alcibiades. A Tragedy*†	1675	Yes	Yes	No	Yes	Ded; Loc implicit; P/Ep
Elkanah Settle	*The Conquest of China. A Tragedy*†	1676	Yes	Yes	No	Yes	Ded; [Loc];[107] P/Ep
Thomas Shadwell	*The Libertine. A Tragedy*†	1676	Yes	Yes	Some	No	Ded; Pref; P/Ep
Thomas Shadwell	*Psyche. A Tragedy*† [also a semi-opera][108]	1675	No	No	No	No	Ded; Pref; P/Ep; [SR]
William Wycherley	*The Country-Wife. A Comedy*†	1675	Yes	No	No	Yes	Loc; P/Ep; [SR]

---

100 Langbaine (1691), p. 545, states that "This Play is only the Tragedy of *Nero Reviv'd*, and printed *verbatim*" (anon.; 1619; pub. 1624).

101 Langbaine (1691), p. 517, says, "P.B. *i.e.* Peter Belon, *Gent*. An Author now living, who is supposed to" have written this play.

102 As Danchin (1981–8) notes, the final speech in Frenchified prose serves as an epilogue (Part I, 2:656–658).

103 This is the first of Dryden's plays to bear a title page license: "Licensed, Roger L'Estrange" (no date).

104 One of the two EEBO copies is misdated "1671."

105 Location from stage directions, not Dramatis Personae.

106 The Dramatis Personae is incomplete and defective in Q1676. Prologue and epilogue are omitted; Q1681 improves the Dramatis Personae and prints a prologue and epilogue used for performances in Oxford that year.

107 Location implicit in title.

108 Adapted from the French tragedie-ballet *Psyché*, produced in Paris in 1671.

Playwright	Title (and genre if stated)	Publication year	List of characters	Connections explained	Characters described	Names of actors given	Other paratext
		Plays premiered in 1676					
Anon. [Rawlins?][109]	Tom Essence. A Comedy*†	1677	Yes	Yes	Yes	Yes	Lic; Loc; P/Ep
Aphra Behn	Abdelazer. A Tragedy*†	1677	Yes	Yes	No	Yes	Loc; P/Ep
Aphra Behn	The Town-Fopp. A Comedy*†	1677	Yes	Yes	No	No	Lic; Loc; P/Ep
Crowne, John	The Countrey Wit. A Comedy†	"1675"[110]	Yes	Yes	Some	Yes	Ded; Loc; P/Ep
Thomas Durfey	The Siege of Memphis. A Tragedy*†	1676	Yes	Yes	No	No	Ded; Loc; P/Ep
Thomas Durfey	Madam Fickle. A Comedy*†	1677	Yes	Yes	No	Yes	Lic; Ded; Loc; P/Ep
Thomas Durfey	The Fool Turn'd Critick. A Comedy†	1678	No	No	No	No	Loc;[111] P/Ep[112]
George Etherege	The Man of Mode. A Comedy*†	1676	Yes	No	No	No[113]	Lic; Ded; Loc implicit; P/Ep; [SR]
Nathaniel Lee	Gloriana**†	1676	Yes	No	No	Yes	Ded; Loc; P/Ep
Thomas Otway	Don Carlos Prince of Spain. A Tragedy†	1676	Yes	Some	No	Yes	Lic; Ded; Pref; Loc; P/Ep; [SR]
Edward Ravenscroft[114]	The Wrangling Lovers. A Comedy*†	1677	Yes	Yes	Some	Yes	Lic; Loc; Ep

109 Langbaine (1691), p. 552, reports that "This Play is said to be writ by One Mr. *Rawlins*."

110 *The Countrey Wit* presents some puzzles. The first known performance was one attended by Charles II on 10 January 1676, but the title page of the first edition is dated 1675. It was not advertised until the Term Catalogue of May 1676. The Duke's Company may have performed the play late in 1675, or the year in the imprint may be misleading.

111 Covent Garden is specified at the beginning of Acts I, II, III, and V.

112 Lyrics and music for songs at pages 16, 35, and 51.

113 We have the cast from Downes, pp. 76–77.

114 The EEBO has two copies. One carries no authorial ascription. The other states on the title page: "Written by Edward Ravenscroft, Gent."

Elkanah Settle	*Ibrahim the Illustrious Bassa. A Tragedy*†	1677	Yes	Some	No	Yes	Lic; Ded; Loc; P/Ep
Elkanah Settle	*Pastor Fido. A Pastoral**†	1677	Yes	Yes	No	Yes	Lic; Ded; Loc; P/Ep;[115] [SR]
Thomas Shadwell	*The Virtuoso. A Comedy*†	1676	Yes	Yes	Yes	No	Lic; Ded; Loc; P/Ep; [SR]
William Wycherley	*The Plain-Dealer. A Comedy*†	1677	Yes	Yes	Yes	Yes	Lic; Ded;[116] Loc; P/Ep
	Plays premiered in 1677						
Anon.[117]	*The Counterfeit Bridegroom. A Comedy**†	1677	Yes	Some	Some	Yes	Lic; Loc; P/Ep
Anon.[118] [adapting Brome]	*The Debauchee. A Comedy**†	1677	Yes	Yes	No	No	Lic; Loc; P/Ep; [SR]
Anon. [adapting Chamberlaine]	*Wits Led by the Nose. A Tragi-Comedy**†	1678	Yes	Yes	Some	Yes	Lic; Loc; P/Ep
John Banks	*The Rival Kings. A Tragedy.**†	1677	Yes	Some	No	No	Ded; Loc; P/Ep; [SR]
Aphra Behn[119]	*The Rover* [Part 1]*††	1677	Yes	Yes	Some	Yes	Lic; Loc; P/Ep; [SR][120]
John Crowne	*The Destruction of Jerusalem by Titus Vespasian* [two parts]*†	1677	Yes	Yes	Some	No[121]	Ded; Epistle to Reader; Loc implicit; P/Ep[122]
Charles Davenant	*Circe. A Tragedy*[semi-opera]†	1677	Yes	Yes	No	No	Lic; Loc; P/Ep; [SR]

115 A different prologue and epilogue were separately published. See Danchin (1981–8), Part I, 2:748–753.

116 The extensive and mocking dedication is "To my LADY B——", a notable brothel keeper described by Pepys as "a famous Strumpet" (*Diary*, 22 September 1660).

117 Langbaine (1691), pp. 528–529, says, "This … is only an Old Play of *Middleton's*, call'd *No Wit like a Woman*." Later scholars have ascribed responsibility for the alterations to Behn and/or Betterton. Mary Ann O'Donnell (2004), pp. 261–262, considers these speculations plausible but unproven.

118 Langbaine (1691), p. 529, says, "This Play is by some ascrib'd to Mrs. *Behn*; but it is indeed only a Play of *Brome's* reviv'd, call'd *A mad Couple well match'd*."

119 The first two plays of the 1677 edition title page do not name an author, but the third says, "Written by Mrs. *A. Behn*." See Plates 1, 2, and 3 and O'Donnell, 2004, A6.1c (pp. 30–34). Elaine Hobby points out to me that the third state is relatively rare and offers the plausible hypothesis that they were created as presentation copies for the author. Of more than thirty known copies of the various states of the 1677 edition, only three are exemplars of the third state.

120 *The Rover* is altogether exceptional in concluding with a "Post-script" of half a page, indignantly rebutting charges of plagiarism. Such addresses to the reader are usually found in the prelims. (See Plates 7a and b for both states of the addendum.)

121 Downes (1987), p. 34, supplies an abbreviated cast.

122 Separate prologue and epilogue for Part 2 (printed out of order). The text of a song is inserted at the end of the prelims of Part 1.

(cont.)

Playwright	Title (and genre if stated)	Publication year	List of characters	Connections explained	Characters described	Names of actors given	Other paratext
John Dryden	All for Love. A Tragedy*†	1678	Yes	Yes	No	Yes	Ded; Pref; Loc; P/Ep; [SR]
Thomas Durfey	A Fond Husband. A Comedy*†	1677	Yes	Yes	Yes	Yes	Lic;[123] Ded; P/Ep
John Leanerd	The Country Innocence. A Comedy*†	1677	Yes	A few	No	Yes	Lic; Ded; To Readers; P/Ep; [SR]
Nathaniel Lee	The Rival Queens**†[124]	1677	Yes	Yes	No	Yes	Ded; Loc; P/Ep[125]
Thomas Otway	Titus and Berenice. A Tragedy[126]	1677	Yes	Some	No	Yes	Ded; Loc; P/Ep[127]
	... With a Farce called the Cheats of Scapin† [two plays]						
Samuel Pordage	The Siege of Babylon*†	1678	Yes	Yes	No	Yes	Lic; Ded; Loc; P/Ep
Sir Charles Sedley	Antony and Cleopatra. A Tragedy†	1677	Yes	No	No	Yes	Lic; Loc implicit; P/Ep; [SR]

123 Elaine Hobby observes to me in correspondence that L'Estrange's title page license date is in fact "June 15. 1676," raising some question about May 1677 as the generally accepted date of premiere. I offer the hypothesis that the L'Estrange date is a typo for "1677." Charles II is said to have attended three of the first five nights, and we have proof of his attendance on 31 May and 8 June 1677. See The London Stage, Part 1, pp. 257–258.

124 No generic label on title page, but the subtitle makes the genre plain: "Or the Death of Alexander the Great."

125 Prelims include "To Mr. Lee, on his Alexander" by John Dryden.

126 Mainpiece and afterpiece published together. The two casts contain no overlap, but specify location for each play (Rome and Dover, respectively).

127 A single prologue and epilogue serve for both parts of the double bill.

Plays premiered in 1678

Author	Play	Year					Paratext
Anon. ["Written by a Person of Quality"][128]	Tunbridge-Wells. A Comedy*†	1678	Yes	Yes	Yes	No	Lic; P/Ep
Anon.[129]	The Counterfeits. A Comedy†	1679	Yes	No	No	Yes	Lic; Loc;[130] P/Ep
Anon. ["A Person of Quality"]	The Constant Nymph. A Pastoral*†	1678	Yes	Yes	No	Yes	Lic; Ded; Loc; P/Ep
T. P. [Thomas Porter?]	The French Conjurer. A Comedy†	1678	Yes	Yes	Some	Yes	Lic; Bookseller to Reader; Loc; P/Ep
John Banks	The Destruction of Troy. A Tragedy†	1679	Yes	Yes	A bit	Yes	Lic; Ded; Loc; P/Ep; [SR]
John Bancroft	The Tragedy of Sertorius†	1679	Yes	Some	A bit	No	Lic; Ded; Loc; P/Ep
Aphra Behn	Sir Patient Fancy. A Comedy†	1678	Yes	Yes	Yes	Yes	Lic; Pref; Loc; P/Ep
John Dryden	The Kind Keeper. A Comedy*†	1680	Yes	Yes	Yes	No	Ded; Loc; P/Ep
John Dryden & Nathaniel Lee	Oedipus. A Tragedy†	1679	Yes	Yes	No	Yes	Lic; Pref; Loc; P/Ep
Thomas Durfey	Trick for Trick. A Comedy*†	1678	Yes	Yes	No	Yes	Lic; P/Ep; Loc implicitly London
Thomas Durfey	Squire Oldsapp. A Comedy*†	1679	Yes	Yes	Yes	Yes	Lic; Loc implicitly London; P/Ep
Edward Howard	The Man of Newmarket*†	1678	Yes	Yes	Yes	Yes	Lic; Induction; Loc;[131] P/Ep
John Leanerd	The Rambling Justice** †	1678	Yes	Yes	Yes	Yes	Lic; Loc; P/Ep

[128] Langbaine (1691), p. 554, says of *Tunbridge-Wells*, "I have been told it was writ by Mr. *Rawlins*."

[129] Langbaine (1691), p. 528, says of *The Counterfeits*, "This Comedy is ascribed by some to *Leanard*; but I believe it too good to be his Writing," pointing to a Spanish source.

[130] Situated in Madrid (specified in act headings).

[131] Title character notwithstanding, "The Scene, *London*."

(cont.)

Playwright	Title (and genre if stated)	Publication year	List of characters	Connections explained	Characters described	Names of actors given	Other paratext
Nathaniel Lee	Mithridates. A Tragedy†	1678[132]	Yes	Yes	No	Yes	Lic; Ded; Loc; P/Ep
Thomas Otway	Friendship in Fashion. A Comedy†	1678	Yes	No	No	Yes	Ded; P/Ep; Loc implicit; P/Ep
Edward Ravenscroft	Scaramouch a Philos-opher. A Comedy*†	1677	Yes	Yes	A bit	Yes	P/Ep
Edward Ravenscroft	King Edgar and Alfreda. A Tragi-Comedy†	1677	Yes	Yes	Some	Yes	Note to Reader;[133] Loc; P/Ep
Edward Ravenscroft	The English Lawyer. A Comedy†[134]	1678	Yes	Yes	No	No	Loc; P/Ep
Thomas Shadwell	The History of Timon of Athens. A Play†	1678	Yes[135]	Some	No	Yes	Lic; Ded; Loc; P/Ep; [SR]
Thomas Shadwell	A True Widow. A Comedy†	1679	Yes	Yes	Yes	No	Ded; Loc; P/Ep
Nahum Tate	Brutus of Alba. A Tragedy*†	1678	Yes	Some	No	No	Lic; Ded; Pref; Loc; P/Ep

132 The EEBO copy of the 1678 *Mithridates* lacks a Dramatis Personae page, but both the Stroup-Cooke edition and Part 1 of *The London Stage* attribute a cast list to that edition that is repeated in Q1685.

133 Followed by an eight-page Life of Edgar.

134 Langbaine (1691), p. 420, reports that this was an adaptation of an English translation of Ruggle's Latin *Ignoramus* published in 1662.

135 The EEBO copy of the 1678 *History of Timon of Athens* lacks a Dramatis Personae page, but Summers' edition of Shadwell (3:197) supplies what I take to be the original cast from a complete copy of the first edition.

		Plays premiered in 1679					
Aphra Behn	The Feign'd Curtizans. A Comedy*†	1679	Yes	Yes	Yes	Yes	Lic; Ded; Loc; P/Ep
Aphra Behn	The Young King*†	1683	Yes	Yes	Yes	No	Ded; Loc; P/Ep
John Crowne	The Ambitious Statesman*††	1679	Yes	Some	Some	No	Ded; Pref; Loc; P/Ep
John Dryden (adapt. Shakespeare)	Troilus and Cressida. A Tragedy*†	1679	Yes	No	No	Yes	Ded; Pref; P/Ep;¹³⁶ [SR]
Thomas Durfey	The Virtuous Wife. A Comedy*†	1680	Yes	Yes	Yes	Yes	Loc; P/Ep
Nathaniel Lee	Caesar Borgia. A Tragedy†	1680	Yes	Yes	No	Yes	Ded; Loc; P/Ep
Thomas Otway	The History and Fall of Caius Marius. A Tragedy†	1680	Yes	No	No	Yes	Ded; Loc implicit; P/Ep
Edward Ravenscroft (adapt. Shakespeare)¹³⁷	Titus Andronicus. A Tragedy*‡	1687	Yes	A few	No	No	Lic; To the Reader; Loc; P/Ep;¹³⁸
Thomas Shadwell	The Woman-Captain. A Comedy†	1680	Yes	Yes	Yes	No	Ded; Loc; P/Ep
Nahum Tate	The Loyal General. A Tragedy†	1680	Yes	No	No	Yes	Ded; Loc; P/Ep

¹³⁶ The location in Troy is implicit but obvious. The dedication runs to six pages in the California Dryden; a meaty critical essay, "The Grounds of Criticism in Tragedy" adds another twenty pages to the five pages of "Preface to the Play."

¹³⁷ Not dateable with much confidence. The *Annals*, 3rd edition, p. 184, says "1679–1686," but this is unnecessarily vague. Ravenscroft's "To the Reader" says that "it first appear'd upon the Stage, at the beginning of the pretended Popish Plot" (i.e., probably in the 1678–9 season).

¹³⁸ Ravenscroft's note to the reader says that "In the Hurry of those distracted times the Prologue and Epilogue were lost: But to let the Buyer have his penny worths, I furnish you with others which were Written by me to other Persons Labours, two of them were proportion'd to that Mad Season." A "Prologue, Spoken before the Long *Vacation*" and "A Prologue after the *Vacation*, Spoken by Mr *Haines*" were added to the prelims. Danchin points out that the prologue and epilogue from Whitaker's *The Conspiracy* (1680) were reused in this play (1981–8), Part 2, 3:230–232, 4:620–626.

Plays published between 1680 and 1689

Playwright	Title (and genre if stated)	Publication year	List of characters	Connections explained	Characters described	Names of actors given	Other paratext
		Plays premiered in 1680					
Anon. [Behn? adapting Marston].[139]	The Revenge. A Comedy*†	1680	Yes	Yes	A bit	Yes	[Loc][140]
John Crowne (adapting Shakespeare).[141]	The Misery of Civil-War: A Tragedy†	1680	Yes	Yes	A bit	Yes	Loc; P/Ep
John Crowne	Thyestes. A Tragedy†	1681	Yes	Yes	No	No	Loc; P/Ep[142]
John Dryden	The Spanish Fryar***	1681	Yes	A bit	No	Yes	Ded; P/Ep
Nathaniel Lee	Lucius Junius Brutus. A Tragedy†	1681	Yes	No	No	Some	Ded; Loc; P/Ep
Nathaniel Lee	Theodosius. A Tragedy*†	1680	Yes	No	No	Partial	Ded; P/Ep[143]
Lewis Maidwell	The Loving Enemies. A Comedy†	1680	Yes	Yes	Some	Yes	Ded; Loc; P/Ep
Thomas Otway	The Orphan. A Tragedy*†	1680	Yes	Yes	No	Yes	Ded; Loc; P/Ep
Thomas Otway	The Souldiers Fortune. A Comedy†	1681	Yes	No	No	Yes	Ded; Loc; P/Ep
Elkanah Settle	Fatal Love. A Tragedy*†	1680	Yes	Yes	No	No	Ded; Loc; P/Ep
Elkanah Settle	The Female Prelate. A Tragedy*†	1680	Yes	Yes	Some	No	Ded; Loc[144]

139 Langbaine (1691), p. 547, says of The Revenge that "This Play is ascrib'd to Mrs. Behn; but it is indeed a Play of Marston's revised, and called The Dutch Curtezan." Later scholars have variously ascribed the alterations to Behn or Betterton. Stylistically Behn is a plausible attribution, though she could certainly have worked with Betterton. Narcissus Luttrell bought a copy on 6 July 1680 (now in the Cambridge University Library) in which he ascribed the play to Behn.

140 Implicit in subtitle: "A Match in Newgate."

141 Shakespeare is acknowledged only in passing in the prologue. For a detailed account of Crowne's utilization of Shakespeare's three Henry VI plays in The Misery of Civil-War and Henry the Sixth: The First Part (1681), see White (1922), pp. 107–118.

142 The text of "The Song at Atreus his Banquet" is interpolated in the prelims after the title page in the EEBO copy.

143 The title page reads "With the Musick betwixt the Acts," and ten pages of text and music of songs performed between the acts are added at the end.

144 Lack of a prologue and epilogue is highly unusual in a professionally performed play published by its author.

Nahum Tate (adapting Shakespeare)	*The History of King Richard the Second*†[145]	1681	Yes	No	No	No	Ded; P/Ep[146]
Nahum Tate (adapt. Shakespeare)	*The History of King Lear*. Reviv'd with Alterations†	1681	Yes	No	No	Yes	Ded; P/Ep
William Whitaker	*The Conspiracy*. A Tragedy*†	1680	Yes	No	No	No	P/Ep
Plays premiered in 1681							
John Banks	*The Unhappy Favourite*. A Tragedy*†	1682	A bit	No	No	Yes	Ded; Loc; P/Ep;[147]
Aphra Behn	*The Rover* [Part 2]*†	1681	Yes	No	No	Yes	Ded; Loc; P/Ep
Aphra Behn	*A Farce Call'd The False Count*†	1682	Yes	Some	Some	Yes	Lic;[148] P/Ep[149]
Aphra Behn [adapt. Tatham, *The Rump*, 1660]	*The Roundheads*. A Comedy*†	1682	Yes	A bit	A bit	No	Ded; [Loc implicit]; P/Ep
John Crowne (adapt. Shakespeare)	*Henry the Sixth the First Part***†	1681	Yes	Yes	A bit	Some	Ded; Loc; P/Ep
Thomas Durfey	*Sir Barnaby Whigg*. A Comedy*†	1681	Yes	Yes	Yes	Yes	Ded; Loc; P/Ep

145 The title page continues: "Acted at the Theatre Royal, Under the Name of the *Sicilian Usurper*. With a Prefatory *Epistle* in Vindication of the Author. Occasion'd by the PROHIBITION of this *PLAY* on the Stage." Unsold copies were reissued by J. Knapton in 1691 with a cancel title page: "*The Sicilian Usurper: A Tragedy*. As it was Acted at the Theatre-Royal."

146 Texts of the songs are published in the prelims.

147 A "Prologue Intended to be spoken, Written by the Author" is added after the epilogue. The prologue printed in the prelims was "Spoken to the King and Queen at their coming to the House, and Written on purpose By Mr. *Dryden*."

148 The title page carries the entry, "Licensed July 21. 1681. *Charles Killigrew*." This is bizarre. Licensing for publication was not in force at this time, and Charles Killigrew was the Master of the Revels, charged with licensing play scripts for performance, not print. Very likely the manuscript submitted to Killigrew for a performance license in June or July 1681 and duly inscribed with his approval was in due course used as copy for the printer, who then set what he found on the title page. The edition was dated "1682" but Luttrell's copy is dated 17 December 1681 and he altered the date of publication from "1682" to "1681." See O'Donnell (2004), p. 50. *The London Stage* dates the play "November 1681" on the basis of the Luttrell copy date, but this is an implausibly short gap between premiere and publication. Premiere in September or October is likely. See Milhous and Hume (1974). Mary Ann O'Donnell kindly informs me that the cancellans state is found only in the Harvard, New York Public Library, and Trinity College Dublin copies. The cancellans version removes both the "Farce" designation and the inappropriate licensing notice. EEBO contains both issues.

149 Location is implied by the description of Don Carlos as "Governour of *Cadez*."

Playwright	Title (and genre if stated)	Publication year	List of characters	Connections explained	Characters described	Names of actors given	Other paratext
Edward Ravenscroft	The London Cuckolds. A Comedy†	[1682]	Yes	Yes	Some	Yes	P/Ep[150]
Charles Saunders	Tamerlane the Great. A Tragedy†	1681	Yes	Some	No	No	Pref;[151] Loc; P/Ep
Thomas Shadwell	The Lancashire Witches. A Comedy*†	1682	Yes	Yes	Yes	No	To the Reader; Loc; P/Ep
Nahum Tate	The Ingratitude of a Common-wealth*†	1682	Yes	Yes	Yes	No	Ded; Loc; P/Ep
	Plays premiered in 1682						
Anon.	Mr Turbulent. A Comedy*†	1682	Yes	Yes	Yes	Yes	Loc; P/Ep
Anon.	Romulus and Hersilia. A Tragedy*†	1683	Yes	Yes	A bit	No	Loc; P/Ep[152]
John Banks	Vertue Betray'd. A Tragedy*†	1682	Yes	No	No	Yes	Ded; Loc; P/Ep
Aphra Behn	The City-Heiress. A Comedy*†	1682	Yes	Yes	Some	Yes	Ded; Loc; P/Ep
John Dryden & Nathaniel Lee	The Duke of Guise. A Tragedy†	1683	Yes	No	No	Yes	Ded; Loc; P/Ep;[153]
Thomas Durfey	The Injured Princess**†	1682	Yes	Yes	Yes	No	Loc; P/Ep
Thomas Durfey	The Royalist. A Comedy†	1682	Yes	Yes	Yes	Yes	Pref; Loc; P/Ep
Nathaniel Lee	The Princess of Cleve*†[154]	1689	Yes	No	No	Some	Ded; Loc; P/Ep[155]
Thomas Otway	Venice Preserv'd. A Tragedy*†	1682	Yes	A few	No	Yes	Ded; Loc implicit; P/Ep

---

150 An illustration was printed in the prelims, highly unusual at this date.

151 The prelims include a commendatory poem by John Banks.

152 The prologue and epilogue by Aphra Behn were separately printed and bought by Luttrell on 8 August 1682. See Danchin (1981–8), Part II, 4:422–425. They were, as Danchin says, "violently Tory," and they led to the arrest of Behn and Lady Slingsby, an actress in the Duke's Company who spoke the epilogue.

153 The California Dryden (XIV, 214–215) adds to the prelims "'Another Epilogue Intended to have been Spoken to the PLAY, before it was forbidden, last Summer. Written by Mr. *Dryden*'" (omitted from Q1-3 and other early editions).

154 Probably performed in December 1682 (as music for the play is dated) or soon thereafter, but not published until 1689. On the dating problems, see Hume (1976c).

155 The prologue and epilogue for Lee's *The Princess of Cleve* are manifestly written for use circa 1689, when the play finally reached the stage. Dryden's original prologue and epilogue intended for use in 1683 were published in Dryden's *Miscellany Poems* of 1684. They are reprinted by Danchin (1981–8), Part II, 4:441–444.

Elkanah Settle	*The Heir of Morocco.* *††	1682	Yes	Some	No	Yes	Ded; P/Ep
Thomas Southerne	*The Loyal Brother.* A Tragedy*††	1682	Yes	Yes	Some	Yes	Ded; Loc implicit; P/Ep
Plays premiered in 1683							
John Crowne	*City Politiques.* A Comedy†	1683	Yes	Yes	Yes	No	To the Reader; Loc;[156] P/Ep
Nathaniel Lee	*Constantine the Great.* A Tragedy†	1684	Yes	No	No	Yes	P/Ep
Thomas Otway	*The Atheist*††	1684	Yes	Yes	No	Yes	Ded; P/Ep
Edward Ravenscroft	*Dame Dobson.* A Comedy*†	1684	Yes	Some	No	Yes[157]	P/Ep
Plays premiered in 1684							
John Lacy	*Sir Hercules Buffoon.* A Comedy*†	1684	Yes	Yes	No	No	P/Ep
Thomas Southerne	*The Disappointment.* A Play*††	1684	Yes	Yes	No	Yes	Ded; Loc; P/Ep
Nahum Tate[158]	*A Duke and no Duke.* A Farce†	1685	Yes	Some	A bit	Yes	Ded; Pref; Loc; P/Ep[159]
John Wilmot, Earl of Rochester (adapt. Fletcher)	*Valentinian.* A Tragedy†	1685	Yes	Some	No	No	Pref;[160] P/Ep[161]

156 "Scene Naples," but with obvious satiric relevance to London and recognizable individuals.
157 *The London Stage*, Part 1, pp. 319–320, reports a full cast from Q1684, but it is not present in the EEBO copy.
158 Langbaine (1691), p. 501, observes that "This Play is founded on Sir Aston Cockain's *Trappolin suppos'd a Prince*" (pub. 1658).
159 Music and words for three songs appended after the epilogue. The 1693 edition adds an important critical essay on farce, based on an Italian source.
160 Rochester having died five years earlier, the preface was by a "Friend" (Robert Wolseley). It runs to more than twenty pages and is an important early account of Rochester's life and writings.
161 Three prologues are supplied, the one for the first day by Aphra Behn, the others anonymous. The third was "intended" to be spoken by Mrs. Barry.

(cont.)

Playwright	Title (and genre if stated)	Publication year	List of characters	Connections explained	Characters described	Names of actors given	Other paratext
		Plays premiered in 1685					
John Crowne	*Sir Courtly Nice. A Comedy*‡†	1685	Yes	Yes	Yes	No	Ded; P/Ep
John Dryden	*Albion and Albanius. An Opera*†	1685	Yes	No	No	No	Pref; P/Ep[162]
Thomas Durfey[163] (adapt. Fletcher)	*A Common-Wealth of Women. A Play*†	1686	Yes	Yes	Some	Yes	Lic; Ded; Loc; P/Ep
Nahum Tate[164] (adapt. Jonson, et al.)	*Cuckolds-Haven. A Farce*‡†	1685	Yes	Yes	Some	Yes	Lic; Ded; Loc; P/Ep
		Plays premiered in 1686					
Aphra Behn	*The Luckey-Chance. A Comedy*‡‡†	1687	Yes	Yes	Some	Yes	Lic; Ded; Pref; Loc; P/Ep; [SR]
Thomas Durfey	*The Banditti. A Play*‡†	1686	Yes	Yes	A bit	Yes	Lic; Ded; Loc; P/Ep
Thomas Jevon[165]	*The Devil of a Wife*‡‡†	1686	Yes	Yes	Some	Yes	Lic; Ded; Pref; P/Ep; [SR]

162 An extensive description of "The Frontispiece" revealed by the raising of the curtain follows the "Names of the Persons Represented." Unique and detailed descriptions of the scenery and machinery are scattered throughout the text and are credited to Betterton by Dryden in his preface.

163 The prologue states that this adaptation of Fletcher has improved the play – a version of *The Sea Voyage* (1622).

164 The dedication and prologue acknowledge indebtedness to Ben Jonson. The play is a revamping of *Eastward Ho!* by Chapman, Jonson, and Marston (1605).

165 There is no attribution on the title page, but Jevon signed the dedication.

		Plays premiered in 1687					
Aphra Behn	*The Emperor of the Moon. A Farce*†	1687	Yes	No	No	Some	Ded; Loc; P/Ep; [SR]
Sir Charles Sedley	*Bellamira. A Comedy**†	1687	Yes	No	No	No	Lic; Pref; P/Ep; [SR]
Nahum Tate [adapt. Fletcher][166]	*The Island-Princess**†	1687	Yes	No	Yes	No	Ded; Loc
		Plays premiered in 1688					
John Crowne	*Darius, King of Persia. A Tragedy*†	1688	Yes	A bit	Yes	No	Ded; Loc; P/Ep; [SR]
Thomas Durfey	*A Fool's Preferment. A Comedy**†	1688	Yes	Some	Yes	Yes	Lic; Ded; Loc; P/Ep[167]
William Mountfort	*The Injur'd Lovers. A Tragedy**†	1688	Yes	Yes	No	Yes	Lic; Ded; Loc; P/Ep
William Mountfort	*The Life and Death of Doctor Faustus, Made into a Farce**†	**1697**	No	No	No	No	None[168]
Thomas Shadwell	*The Squire of Alsatia. A Comedy*†	1688	Yes	Yes	Yes	Yes	Ded; P/Ep[169]
		Plays premiered in 1689					
Aphra Behn	*The Widdow Ranter. A Tragi-Comedy**†	1690	Yes	Some	Some	Yes	See note[170]
James Carlile	*The Fortune-Hunters. A Comedy**†	1689	Yes	Yes	A bit	Yes	P/Ep; Loc[171]

166 Fletcher is not named in the prelims, but the title page indicates that this is a revamped, not an original play: "With the Alterations and New Additional Scenes."

167 Text and music for eight songs are appended to the text, separately paginated. They are specially proclaimed on the title page: "Together with all the SONGS and NOTES to 'em. Excellently Compos'd by Mr. Henry Purcell. 1688."

168 This short farce (twenty-six pages) was presumably an afterpiece, not published in Mountfort's lifetime. *The London Stage* editors place its premiere tentatively in the season of 1685–6 (Part 1, p. 342) but there is potent evidence suggesting a premiere circa March 1688 shortly after Mountfort's *The Injur'd Lovers*. See Hume (1976b).

169 The location is implicitly London. The prelims include "An Explanation of the Cant," helpfully defining some forty-five slang expressions used in the play.

170 Behn died before the play was performed or printed. The dedication was signed G. J. (George Jenkins?). The location ("Virginia in Bacons Camp") was appended to the Dramatis Personae. A prologue and epilogue by Dryden were separately published at the time of the premiere, but the prologue and epilogue printed with the text of Behn's play were taken without acknowledgment from printed sources in the 1670s. On this tangle, see Danchin (1981–8), Part II, 4:758–765.

171 The texts of two songs are appended to the play.

(cont.)

Playwright	Title (and genre if stated)	Publication year	List of characters	Connections explained	Characters described	Names of actors given	Other paratext
John Dryden	Don Sebastian. A Tragedy†	1690	Yes	Yes	A bit	Yes	Ded; Pref.; Loc; P/Ep;[172] [SR]
Nathaniel Lee	The Massacre of Paris. A Tragedy[173]†	1690	Yes	No	No	Principals	Loc implicit; P/Ep
William Mountfort	The Successful Straingers. A Tragi-Comedy†	1690	Yes	Yes	Some	Yes	Lic; Ded; Pref; Loc; P/Ep; [SR]
Thomas Shadwell	Bury-Fair. A Comedy†	1689	Yes	Some	No	Yes	Ded; Loc; P/Ep

[172] A "Prologue, Sent to the Authour by an unknown hand, and propos'd to be spoken By Mrs. Montfort drest like an Officer" is included in the prelims.

[173] Probably written circa 1679 but not performed because of its toxic political implications at the time of the Popish Plot uproar. It was performed in November 1689 with a prologue and epilogue addressing current events written by Mountfort and Powell, respectively. On a rather different "Prologue. To the Massacre of Paris: For Mr. Betterton," see Danchin (1981–8), Part II, 4:747–754.

Plays published between 1690 and 1699

Playwright	Title (and genre if stated)	Publication year	List of characters in 1690	Connections explained	Characters described	Names of actors given	Other paratext
		Plays premiered in 1690					
Anon. [Thomas Betterton][174]	*The Prophetess* [semi opera]*†	1690	Yes	Some	Some	No	Loc;[175] Ep
Anon.[176]	*King Edward the Third. An Historicall Play*†	1691	Yes	A bit	No	Yes	Ded; Loc; P/Ep
John Crowne	*The English Frier. A Comedy*†	1690	Yes	Yes	Some	Yes	Ded; Pref; Loc; P/Ep
John Dryden	*Amphitryon. A Comedy*†	1690	Yes	No	No	Yes	Ded; P/Ep[177]
Jos. Harris; one scene by Mountfort	*The Mistakes. A Tragi-Comedy*†	1691	Yes	Some	No	Yes	Lic; Ded; Pref; Loc; P/Ep[178]
George Powell	*Alphonso King of Naples. A Tragedy*†	1691	Yes	Yes	No	Yes	Ded; Loc; P/Ep
George Powell	*The Treacherous Brothers. A Tragedy*†	1690	Yes	Yes	No	Yes	Lic; Ded; Pref; Loc; P/Ep;[179] [SR]

174 The title page says: "Written by *Francis Beaumont* and *John Fletcher*. With Alterations and Additions, After the Manner of an Opera." Downes says "an Opera, wrote by Mr. Betterton" (1987, p. 89).

175 The subtitle, *The History of Dioclesian*, locates the setting in Rome during Dioclesian's time as emperor, AD 284–305.

176 *King Edward the Third*, staged by the United Company circa November 1690, presents attributional problems that seem likely to remain permanently insoluble. The title page offers no attribution. William Mountfort signed the dedication and says that the play was "a present to me."

177 The title page states, "To which is added, The Musick of the SONGS. Compos'd by Mr. *Henry* Purcell." Thirteen pages of words to songs and the music by Henry Purcell are appended to this volume (with a separate title page).

178 The prelims contain an elaborate prologue "Writ by Mr. *Dryden*" and delivered by Bright, Bowen, and Williams. Plus an "Epilogue Writ by Mr. *N. Tate*" and "Spoken by Mrs. *Butler* in Mans Cloaths." After the end of Act V is appended an "Epilogue Spoken by Mr. *Montfort*."

179 The prelims include a short compliment in Latin verse signed by Powell's colleague, John Hodgson.

Playwright	Title (and genre if stated)	Publication year	List of characters	Connections explained	Characters described	Names of actors given	Other paratext
Elkanah Settle	Distress'd Innocence: or, The Princess of Persia. A Tragedy*†	1691	Yes	Yes	Some	Yes	Ded; Loc; Ep; [SR]
Thomas Shadwell	The Amorous Bigotte. A Comedy[180]*†	1690	Yes	Yes	Yes	Yes	Ded; Loc; P/Ep
Thomas Shadwell	The Scowrers. A Comedy†	1691	Yes	Yes	A bit	Yes	P/Ep
Thomas Southerne	Sir Anthony Love. A Comedy*†	1691	Yes	A bit	No	Yes	Ded; Loc; P/Ep
		Plays premiered in 1691					
Anon.[181] [John Smythe?]	Win her and Take her. A Comedy*†	1691	Yes	Yes	Yes	No	Ded; P/Ep
John Dryden	King Arthur. A Dramatick Opera*†	1691	Yes	Some	Some	Yes	Ded; Loc; P/Ep[182]
Thomas Durfey (adapting Chapman)[183]	Bussy D'Ambois. A Tragedy*†	1691	Yes	Yes	No	Yes	Ded; Loc; P/Ep; [SR]
Thomas Durfey	Love for Money. A Comedy*†	1691	Yes	Yes	Yes[184]	Yes	Ded; Pref; Loc; P/Ep; [SR]

180 Shadwell says in his prologue that hostile members of the audience may say that this is merely "a damn'd old Play," but that it is massively revised, "like Drake's Ship, 'tis so repair'd 'tis new." The play has recently been shown to be an anonymous reworking of Feniza or The Ingeniouse Mayde, itself a reworking in English of Lope de Vega's La discreta enamorada (1606), evidently performed in London (ca. 1670?) but not published, discovered in a unique manuscript in the University of Chicago Library. For extensive discussion, see Hume (2013).

181 Not attributed on the title page. A fulsome dedication to the Earl of Danby is signed by Cave Underhill, who claims no credit for the play but evidently saw it to the stage. Attributed to John Smyth who got a degree from Magdalen College, Oxford, and became usher of a school attached to that college, by Anthony à Wood, Athenæ Oxonienses, IV, 601.

182 Opposite the title page, Dryden supplies "a Catalogue of my Plays and Poems in Quarto, putting the Plays in the Order I wrote them." Significantly, this list does not include The Indian-Queen. Why this valuable document, signed by Dryden, was ignored and omitted from Volume XVI of the California Dryden in 1996 I fail to understand.

183 The title page reads: "Bussy D'Ambois . . . Newly Revised by Mr. D'Urfey" and the dedication names Chapman.

184 The extent and detail of the character descriptions is extraordinary for the late seventeenth century.

Author	Title	Year					Paratext
William Mountfort	Greenwich-Park. A Comedy†	1691	Yes	Yes	Yes	Yes	Ded; Loc; P/Ep
Thomas Southerne	The Wives Excuse. A Comedy*†	1692	Yes	A few	No	Yes	Ded; Loc; P/Ep[185]
		Plays premiered in 1692					
Anon.[186]	Henry the Second, King of England. A Tragedy*†	1693	Yes	A few	No	Yes	Ded; Loc; P/Ep
Anon. [adapt. Shakespeare]	The Fairy-Queen[187] An Opera†	1692	Yes	Some	No	No	Pref; P; [SR]
Anon. [Nicholas Brady?][188]	The Rape. A Tragedy*†	1692	Yes	No	No	Yes	Ded; P/Ep
John Crowne	Regulus. A Tragedy†	1694	Yes	Yes	Yes	Yes	Loc; P/Ep
John Dryden[189]	Cleomenes, the Spartan-Heroe. A Tragedy†	1692	Yes	Yes	No	Yes	Ded; Pref; Loc; P/Ep[190]
Thomas Durfey	The Marriage-Hater Match'd. A Comedy†	1692	Yes	Yes	Yes	Yes	Ded; Loc; P/Ep[191]
Thomas Shadwell	The Volunteers. A Comedy*†	1693	Yes	Yes	Yes	Yes	Ded;[192] P/Ep

185 The prelims contain a commendatory/consolatory poem by Dryden. Southerne's play, much admired and praised by present-day critics, failed disastrously in the theatre in 1691 and was never revived until the late twentieth century.

186 Brought to the stage by Mountfort, who signed the dedication. Gildon [1699], p. 5, attributes the play to John Bancroft. Harbage (1940) offers the plausible hypothesis that the play was adapted from a lost Henry II by Robert Davenport (1624), entered in the Stationers'' Register in 1653 but now lost (311).

187 Adaptation based on Shakespeare's A Midsummer Night's Dream (though neither Shakespeare nor the play is named in the quarto) as a super-elaborately staged opera. It has been implausibly attributed to a variety of librettists. For an argument that there is no basis for attributing the concoction of the libretto but that Betterton was probably responsible for the elaborate scenery and staging, see Milhous and Hume (1974), p. 15.

188 The quarto supplies no hint of authorship. Gildon ([1699], 167) says the piece "was writ by a Divine" without naming him. David Erskine Baker (1764) supplies "Dr. Brady," and Isaac Reed adds "Nicholas" and some details of his ecclesiastical career in his 1782 revision and updating of Baker's Biographia Dramatica, 1:40–41. The attribution is accepted by the usually trustworthy James Sambrook in his Brady entry in the Oxford Dictionary of National Biography.

189 Thomas Southerne states in his dedication of The Wives Excuse (pub. 1692) that upon Dryden "falling Sick last Summer, he bequeath'd to my care the Writing of half the last Act of his Tragedy of Cleomenes."

190 The prelims contain a commendatory poem by Theophilus Parsons.

191 The prologue and "A Scotch Song in the Third Act" follow the epilogue at the end.

192 To the Queen by Anne Shadwell on behalf of her recently deceased husband. The prelims also include "A Prologue Written by Mr. Shadwell, and designed to be Spoken, but was lost when the Play was Acted."

(cont.)

Playwright	Title (and genre if stated)	Publication year	List of characters	Connections explained	Characters described	Names of actors given	Other paratext
		Plays premiered in 1693					
William Congreve	The Old Batchelour: A Comedy†	1693	Yes	Yes	A bit	Yes	Ded; P/Ep; Loc[193]
William Congreve	The Double-Dealer: A Comedy†	1694	Yes	Yes	Some	Yes	Ded; P/Ep[194]
Thomas Durfey	The Richmond Heiress. A Comedy*†	1693	Yes	Yes	Yes	Yes	Ded; Loc; P/Ep[195]
Henry Higden	The Wary Widow. A Comedy*†	1693	Yes	Yes	Yes	No	Ded; Pref; P/Ep[196]
George Powell[197]	A Very Good Wife. A Comedy†	1693	Yes	Yes	Yes	Yes	Ded; Loc; P/Ep
Thomas Southerne	The Maids last Prayer: A Comedy*†	1693	Yes	Some	No	Yes	Ded; Loc; P/Ep
"Thomas Wright"[198]	The Female Vertuoso's. A Comedy†	1693	Yes	Yes	A bit	Yes	Ded; Loc; P/Ep
		Plays premiered in 1694					
Anon. [Peter Motteux?]	The Rape of Europa by Jupiter.[199] A Masque†	1694	Yes	No	No	Yes[200]	Argument; Loc implicit
John Crowne	The Married Beau. A Comedy*†	1694	Yes	Yes	Yes	No	Ded; Epistle; Loc; P/Ep

---

193 The prelims include commendatory poems by Thomas Southerne, J. Marsh, and Bevil Higgons.

194 The prelims include a ringing commendatory poem by Dryden "To my Dear Friend Mr. Congreve, On His Comedy, call'd 'The Double-Dealer.'"

195 The words for three songs are printed at the end of the prelims.

196 Six commendatory poems are printed in the prelims. The words of three songs are printed before the epilogue at the end.

197 The title page does not ascribe authorship, but George Powell signed the dedication and speaks as playwright.

198 The title page says "Written by Mr. Thomas Wright," but the dedication states that the play was "drawn some years ago from the great Original of French comedy by an Ingenious friend of mine," but now has been "by my Importunities, extorted from him." What Wright contributed if anything is undeterminable. The play is a London-set Anglicization of Molière's Les Femmes savants.

199 Masque with music by John Eccles. Authorship has been the subject of confusion. The London Stage says that "The author is not known" (Part 1, 427). Eugene Haun (1971), p. 145, attributes it to one "William Ranson," citing Wing as his source, but this is a misreading, on which see Hume (1999), p. 96. As of March 2020, the ESTC says that the piece is "Signed on A4v: SC," but this is a misreading of a catchword: the next page starts "Scene." Stoddard Lincoln (1963) argues that the librettist was Peter Anthony Motteux (pp. 140–141, 219–221), an attribution Lucyle Hook accepted in her introduction to the Augustan Reprint Society facsimile. Motteux is a plausible candidate but I am aware of no hard evidence. Some of Eccles' music survives in British Library Add. MS 35043.

200 Plus the names of seven dancers.

Author	Title	Date					
John Dryden	Love Triumphant. A Tragi-Comedy*†	1694	Yes	Yes	No	Yes	Ded; Loc; P/Ep
Thomas Durfey	The Comical History of Don Quixote (Part 1)†	1694	Yes	Some	Yes	Yes	Ded; Loc; P/Ep
Thomas Durfey	The Comical History of Don Quixote (Part 2)†	1694	Yes	Yes	Yes	Yes	Ded (in verse); Pref; P/Ep
Edward Ravenscroft	The Canterbury Guests. A Comedy*†	1695	Yes	Yes	Some	Yes	Ded; Loc; P/Ep
Elkanah Settle	The Ambitious Slave*†	1694	Yes	Yes	No	Yes	Ded; Loc; P/Ep
Thomas Southerne	The Fatal Marriage. A Play*†	1694	Yes	Yes	No	Yes	Ded; Loc; P/Ep

Plays premiered in 1695

Licensing lapsed on 3 May 1695.

No play bearing a 1695 date seems to have been licensed.

Author	Title	Date					
Anon. (adapt. Fletcher)[201]	Bonduca: or; The British Heroine. A Tragedy†	1696	Yes	Yes	No	Yes	Ded; To the Reader; [Loc]; P/Ep
Anon. ("Written [sic] by a Young Lady")[202]	She Ventures, and He Wins. A Comedy†	1696	Yes	Yes	A bit	Yes	Pref; P/Ep
Anon. (Written by a Young Lady)[203]	Agnes de Castro. A Tragedy†	1696	No	Yes	No	Yes	Ded; Loc; P/Ep[204]

---

201 Dedication signed by George Powell, who says in a note "To the Reader" that the adaptation from a Fletcher play was done by "a Friend of mine." The location is implicitly Roman Britain.

202 The preface is signed "Ariadne."

203 Ascribed to Catharine Trotter by Jacob in *The Poetical Register*, p. 260. I suspect that the ultimate source is Gildon's 1699 continuation of Langbaine (1691). *Agnes de Castro* appears neither under "Trotter" nor under title in the index. But it does appear in "The Appendix" of recent work from "Known Authors" attributed (together with Trotter's *Fatal Friendship* of 1698) to "Mrs. Catharine Trotter [sic]."

204 The prelims include a commendatory poem by Delarivier Manley and a prologue "Written by Mr Wycherly *at the Author's Request: Design'd to be Spoke*."

Playwright	Title (and genre if stated)	Publication year	List of characters	Connections explained	Characters described	Names of actors given	Other paratext
Anon. [George Granville][205]	*The She-Gallants. A Comedy*†	1696	Yes	Yes	A bit	Yes	Pref; Loc; P/Ep
John Banks	*Cyrus the Great: or the Tragedy of Love**†	1696	Yes	Yes	No	Yes	Ded; Loc; P/Ep
William Congreve	*Love for Love. A Comedy*†	1695	Yes	Yes	Yes	Yes	Ded; Loc; P/Ep[206]
Thomas Dilke	*The Lover's Luck. A Comedy*†	1696	Yes	Yes	Yes	Yes	Ded; Loc; P/Ep
Thomas Durfey	*The Comical History of Don Quixote. The Third Part**‡[207]	1696	Yes	Yes	Some	Yes	Ded; Pref; P/Ep
Robert Gould	*The Rival Sisters. A Tragedy**‡†	1696	Yes	Yes	No	Yes	Ded; Loc; P/Ep
Charles Hopkins	*Pyrrhus King of Epirus. A Tragedy*†	1695	Yes	Yes	No	No	Ded; Loc; P/Ep;[208]
Peter Motteux	*The Taking of Namur*[209]*‡†	[1695?]	No	No	No	No	None
Thomas Scott	*The Mock-Marriage. A Comedy*†	1696	Yes	Yes	No	Yes	Pref; Loc; P/Ep
Elkanah Settle[210] (adapt. Beaumont & Fletcher)	*Philaster. A Tragi-Comedy*[211]*‡†	1695	Yes	No	No	Yes	Ded; Loc; P/Ep
Thomas Southerne	*Oroonoko. A Tragedy*†	1696	Yes	Some	No	Yes	Ded; Loc; P/Ep

205 Attributed to George Granville (later Lord Lansdowne) by Gildon [1699], p. 66, confirmed by Downes (1987), p. 94. The "Preface to the Reader" claims that the author wrote the play "in *France* about twelve Years Past" – that is, circa 1684, when Granville would have been just seventeen. Since the source was Campistron's *L'Amante Amant*, acted in 1684, this is possible.

206 The prelims include "A Prologue for The opening of the new Play-House, propos'd to be spoken by Mrs. *Bracegirdle* in Man's Cloaths," and a "Prologue Spoken at the opening of the New House, By Mr. *Betterton*."

207 Lack of company/venue credit on the title page of the EEBO copy is altogether exceptional. As with Parts 1 and 2, Part 3 was mounted by the Patent Company at Drury Lane.

208 Location specified at the beginning of I.i.

209 An interpolated entertainment or afterpiece staged at Lincoln's Inn Fields in September or October 1695: "*Words for a Musical Entertainment at the New-Theatre, Little Lincolns Inn Fields; on The Taking of Namur, and His Majesty's Safe Return*. Set to Music by Mr. *John Eccles*. Written by Mr. *Motteux*." Not noticed in *The London Stage*.

210 Not attributed on the title page, but Settle signed the dedication and credits himself with the alterations.

211 "Revis'd, and the Two last Acts new Written."

Plays premiered in 1696

Anon. [John Vanbrugh][212]	The Relapse. A Comedy*†	1697	Yes	Yes	Minimally	Minimally	Pref; P/Ep[213]
Anon. [John Vanbrugh]	I Æsop.[214] A Comedy†	1697	Yes	Some	Minimally	Minimally	Pref; P
Anon.[215]	A New Opera called, Brutus of Alba*†	1697	Yes	No	No	No	Ded; P/Ep[216]
Anon.[217]	The Cornish Comedy†	1696	Yes	Yes	Yes	Yes	Ded; Pref; Loc; P/Ep
Anon. ("Mr. W. M.")[218]	The Female Wits. A Comedy*†	1704	Yes	Yes	Yes	Yes	Pref; Loc implicit (the theatre); P/Ep
Anon.[219]	Neglected Virtue. A Play*†	1696	Yes	Yes	No	No	Ded; Loc; P/Ep
Anon. ("a Person of Quality")[220]	Pausanias the Betrayer of His Country. A Tragedy†	1696	Yes	Some	A bit	A bit	Ded; Loc; P/Ep

212 Treating The Relapse as anonymous may seem disconcerting, but is accurate. Nothing by Vanbrugh was published in England naming him as the author prior to 1719. See Hume, "The Strange Anonymity of John Vanbrugh," forthcoming in Huntington Library Quarterly.

213 A "Prologue on the Third Day" is added to the prelims.

214 Part I of Aesop was probably premiered in January 1697 and published shortly thereafter. It concludes with a lengthy speech in verse by the title character, which serves as an epilogue of sorts. Part II was added as a kind of continuation/afterpiece circa March 1697 and published together with the second edition of Part I (sixteen pages, separately paginated). It does not have separate paratext. The anonymous playwright (Vanbrugh) announces in his preface that the play is a loose and expanded translation of Edmé Boursault's Aesop – that is, Ésope à la Ville (1690).

215 The dedication to Sam. Briscoe (the publisher) is signed by George Powell and John Verbruggen, who evidently shared two benefits. Whether these actors were responsible for the operatic alterations I see no way to determine.

216 Some copies lack the prologue and epilogue, but they are present in others. See Danchin (1981–8), Part III, 6:323–326.

217 Brought to the stage by George Powell, who signed the dedication to Christopher Rich. Powell states that the script was "committed by the Author to my Hand to Dispose in the World."

218 Said on the title page to be "Written by Mr. W. M.," who remains unidentified. See the facsimile reprint with introduction by Lucyle Hook (1967). Hook notes that the topical prologue and epilogue were added at the time of publication, nearly eight years later. Usually regarded as a committee enterprise, very possibly headed by Jo Hayns.

219 Dedication signed by Hildeband Horden on behalf of a "Friend."

220 Brought to the stage by Thomas Southerne, who signed the dedication. The play was praised by Dr. Samuel Garth near the end of Canto IV of The Dispensary (1699 and oft reprinted). The author is identified as Richard Norton (1666–1732) in later "Keys" to the poem, an attribution accepted by Jordan and Love in their edition of The Works of Thomas Southerne, 2:483.

(cont.)

Playwright	Title (and genre if stated)	Publication year	List of characters	Connections explained	Characters described	Names of actors given	Other paratext
Anon. [Charles Gildon][221]	The Roman Brides Revenge. A Tragedy†	1697	Yes	Yes	A bit	No	Ded; P/Ep
Aphra Behn[222]	The Younger Brother. A Comedy*††	1696	Yes	No	No	Yes	P/Ep and see note 228
Colley Cibber	Love's Last Shift. A Comedy*††	1696	Yes	Yes	Yes	Yes	Ded; Loc; P/Ep
Colley Cibber	Womans Wit. A Comedy*†	1697	Yes	Yes	A bit	Yes	Pref; Loc; P/Ep
Thomas Doggett	The Country-Wake. A Comedy†	1696	Yes	No	No	Yes	Ded; Loc; P/Ep
John Dryden, Jun.	The Husband His Own Cuckold. A Comedy†	1696	Yes	Some	No	No	Ded; Pref;[223] P/Ep[224]
Joseph Harris (adapt. Webster)[225]	The City Bride. A Comedy*†	1696	Yes	Yes	No	Yes	Ded; Loc; P
Delariviere Manley	The Lost Lover. A Comedy*†	1696	Yes	Some	A bit	Yes	Pref; Loc; P/Ep
Delariviere Manley	The Royal Mischief. A Tragedy†	1696	Yes	Some	No	Yes	Ded; To the Reader; Loc; P/Ep
Peter Motteux	Love's a Jest. A Comedy†	1696	Yes	Yes	No	Yes	Ded; Pref; Loc; P/Ep

[221] Gildon credits the play to himself in 1699 in his (anonymous) Lives and Characters, p. 176.
[222] Behn died in 1689. This play was brought to the stage and published seven years after her death by Charles Gildon, who signed the dedication and admitted that he was responsible for "Alterations" including "removing that old bustle about Whigg and Tory." A two-page "Account of the Life of the Incomparable Mrs. BEHN" is not attributed.
[223] Signed by the father, not the son.
[224] A "Dialogue" between husband and wife takes the place of the usual epilogue.
[225] The title page carries no attribution, but Joseph Harris signed the dedication, representing the play as his work.

Peter Motteux	*The Loves of Mars & Venus* [a/p]. "A Play set to Music"†	1696	Yes	A bit	No	Some	Ded; Pref; P/Ep²²⁶
Mary Pix	*Ibrahim, the Thirteenth Emperor of the Turks. A Tragedy*†	1696	Yes	Yes	No	Yes	Ded; Pref; P/Ep
Mary Pix	*The Spanish Wives. A Farce*†	1696	Yes	Yes	Yes	No	Ded; Loc; P/Ep
	Plays premiered in 1697						
Anon.	*The Triumphs of Virtue.* A Tragi-Comedy†	1697	Yes	Yes	No	Yes	P/Ep
Anon. [Dr James Drake]²²⁷	*The Sham-Lawyer**†‡²²⁸	1697	Yes	Yes	Yes	Yes	P/Ep
Anon. ("Ariadne")	*The Unnatural Mother**†	1698	Yes	Yes	No	No	Loc; P/Ep
Anon. [John Vanbrugh]	*The Provok'd Wife.* A Comedy†	1698	Yes	A bit	No	Yes	P/Ep
William Congreve	*The Mourning Bride.* A Tragedy†	1697	Yes	Yes	A bit	Yes	Ded; Loc; P/Ep
John Dennis	*A Plot and no Plot.* A Comedy†	[1697]	Yes	Yes	No	Yes	Ded; Advertise-ment to the Reader; Loc; P/Ep
Thomas Dilke	*The City Lady.* A Comedy*†	1697	Yes	Yes	Yes	Yes	Ded; Loc; P/Ep
Thomas Durfey	*The Intrigues at Versailles.* A Comedy*†	1697	Yes	Yes	Yes	Yes	Ded; Loc; P/Ep
Thomas Durfey	*A New Opera, call'd Cinthia and Endimion**†‡²²⁹	1697	Yes	No	No	No	Ded; Loc; P/Ep

226 A two-page "Explanation of the Fable" from Motteux's *Gentleman's Journal* is appended at the end.

227 Attributed by Gildon [1699], p. 40, to Dr James Drake, "A member of the College of Physitians, and formerly of *Gonville* and *Caius College* in *Cambridge*."

228 The title page announces: "As it was Damnably ACTED at the Theatre-Royal In *Drury-Lane*."

229 *Cinthia and Endimion* is a unique and peculiar case. The *Annals* places it under 1684 and says, "c. 1684–1694 perf. Dec. 1696–Jan. 1697." Two songs used in the opera were published in *The Theater of Music* as early as 1685, but all other evidence points to composition in 1694. The title page says "As it was Design'd to be Acted at Court, before the late QUEEN; and is now Acted at the Theatre Royal, by His Majesty's Servants." Queen Mary died in December 1694. Publication occurred in 1697. The Library of Congress copy is dated "16 Januar." [1697].

(cont.)

Playwright	Title (and genre if stated)	Publication year	List of characters	Connections explained	Characters described	Names of actors given	Other paratext
Edward Filmer[230]	The Unnatural Brother. A Tragedy†	1697	Yes	Yes	No	No	Pref; Loc; P/Ep
George Granville	Heroick Love. A Tragedy†	1698	Yes	Yes	No	Yes	Pref; Loc; P/Ep[231]
Charles Hopkins	Boadicea Queen of Britain. A Tragedy†	1697	Yes	Yes	No	Yes	Ded;[232] Loc; P/Ep
Peter Motteux	Europe's Revels for the Peace. A Musical Interlude[a/p]‡†[233]	1697	Yes	No	No	Yes	Ded; P/Ep[234]
Motteux et al.	The Novelty. Every Act a Play[235]†	1697	Yes[236]	Varies	No	Yes	Ded; Pref; Loc; P/Ep
Mary Pix[237]	The Deceiver Deceived. A Comedy†	1698	Yes	Yes	A bit	Yes	Ded; P/Ep[238]
Mary Pix	The Innocent Mistress. A Comedy†	1697	Yes	Yes	Some	Yes	P/Ep
George Powell[239]	The Imposture Defeated. A Comedy*†	1698	Yes	No	No	Yes	To the Reader; P/Ep
Edward Ravenscroft	The Italian Husband. A Tragedy†	1698	Yes	Some	No	Yes	Ded; P/Ep[240]

230 There is no attribution on the title page, but Filmer signed the preface and claimed the play.

231 A commendatory poem by Dryden is added to the prelims.

232 In verse (highly unusual) to Congreve.   233   "Set to Musick by Mr. John Eccles" (p. 1).

234 "A Panegyrical Poem on His Majesty" serves as a prologue. A "Grand Chorus" serves as epilogue, followed by "Words for a single Song on the Kings Return. Design'd for a Private Performance."

235 "A Short Pastoral, Comedy, Masque, Tragedy, and Farce after the Italian manner." A medley of short pieces by Motteux, Oldmixon, and Filmer.

236 Listed separately with each act.

237 No author is credited on the title page, but Pix signed the dedication.

238 A second epilogue "Design'd for Mr. Verbruggen" is appended. Fourth- and fifth-act dialogues are interpolated into the prelims.

239 Powell is not credited on the title page, but he signed the dedication and denied stealing a character from "a Comedy of Mrs. P—t's" (a playwright I have not been able to identify, said to have "carry'd the Play to the other House").

240 The prologue is preceded by a three-person "Prælude" of four pages.

Author	Title	Year					Paratext
Thomas Scott (adapt. Fletcher)[241]	*The Unhappy Kindness. A Tragedy**†	1697	Yes	A bit	A bit	Yes	Pref; P/Ep[242]
Elkanah Settle[243]	*The World in the Moon. An Opera*†	1697	Yes	Yes	A bit	Yes	Ded; [Loc];[244] P/Ep
Plays premiered in 1698[245]							
Anon.[246]	*The Fatal Discovery. A Tragedy**†	1698	Yes	No	No	Yes	Pref; P
Anon. [Charles Gildon][247]	*Phaeton. A Tragedy*[248]*†	1698	Yes	Yes	No	Yes	Ded; Pref; Loc; P/Ep
John Crowne	*Caligula. A Tragedy*†[249]	1698	Yes	Yes	A bit	Yes	Ded; Epistle to the Reader; Loc; P/Ep
John Dennis	*Rinaldo and Armida* [semi-opera]. A Tragedy[250]†	1699	Yes	No	No	Yes	Ded; Pref; Loc; P/Ep

241 The preface describes the adaptation in some detail, and the prologue mentions Fletcher without naming the original play. Gildon ([1699], p. 122) says, "This Play is only the *Wife for a Month* of *Fletcher*'s alter'd."

242 "The Epilogue written, and spoken by, Mr. *Haynes*, in the Habit of a *Horse Officer*, mounted on an *Ass*." The location is implied by the presence of "*Alphonso*, King of *Naples*" and "*Frederick*, his Brother and Usurper."

243 The title page says merely "By E. S." but the Dedication to Christopher Rich is signed "E. Settle."

244 The setting is basically the Dorset Garden theatre and its environs.

245 Vanbrugh's translation of Dancourt's *La maison de campagne* as *The Country-House* (an afterpiece) was attended by Lady Morley on 18 January 1698 but not published until 1715 and was not associated with Vanbrugh until the edition of 1735. It has no paratext pertinent to the 1690s.

246 Preface signed by George Powell, who calls the author "unknown." Most of Powell's preface is devoted to a hysterically violent denunciation of John Dryden's "To *Mr. Granville*, on his Excellent Tragedy, call'd *Heroick Love*," printed in the prelims of Granville's play.

247 Attributed to Gildon in his own *The Lives and Characters of the English Dramatick Poets* (itself published without attribution), pp. 175–176.

248 Described on the title page as an "Imitation of the Antients."

249 In the EEBO copy, title page and Epistle to Reader occupy A1–4; Prologue, Epilogue, Persons, and a list of other books published by Wellington occupy [H3r-H4v], following "Finis" at the end of Act V.

250 The lyrics (but not the music) were published separately in *The Musical Entertainments in the Tragedy of Rinaldo and Armida* (1699), "All composed by Mr. John Eccles, and Writ by Mr. Dennis." Both were published by Tonson.

(cont.)

Playwright	Title (and genre if stated)	Publication year	List of characters	Connections explained	Characters described	Names of actors given	Other paratext
Thomas Dilke	*The Pretenders*. A Comedy*†	1698	Yes	Yes	Yes	Yes	Ded; Loc; P/Ep
Thomas Durfey	*The Campaigners*. A Comedy*‡[251]	1698	Yes	Yes	A bit	Yes	Ded; P/Ep; Pref;[252]
George Farquhar	*Love and a Bottle*. A Comedy†	1699	Yes	Yes	Some	Yes	Ded; Loc; P/Ep
Peter Motteux	*Beauty in Distress*. A Tragedy†	1698	Yes	Yes	A bit	Yes	Ded; Pref; Loc; P/Ep[253]
John Oldmixon (trans. Tasso)	*Amintas*. A Pastoral†	1698	Yes	No	No	No	Pref; P/Ep
William Phillips	*The Revengeful Queen*. A Tragedy†	1698	Yes	A bit	A bit	No	Ded; [Loc];[254] P/Ep
Mary Pix	*Queen Catharine*. A Tragedy*†	1698	Yes	Yes	No	Yes	Ded; P/Ep
Catherine Trotter[255]	*Fatal Friendship*. A Tragedy†	1698	Yes	Yes	No	Yes	Ded; P/Ep
William Walker	*Victorious Love*. A Tragedy†	1698	Yes	Yes	No	No	Ded; Pref;[256] Loc; P/Ep

251 Lack of indication of company and theatre auspices is extraordinary and must simply have been a mistake. The cast proves that the play was mounted by the patent company at Drury Lane.

252 A twenty-seven-page "Preface" denounces Jeremy Collier and his *A Short View of the Immorality and Profaneness of The English Stage* (1698). It is followed by a five-page verse "Fable" titled "The Dog and the Otter."

253 The prelims include "A Letter from a Divine of the Church of England, To the Author of the Tragedy call'd *Beauty in Distress*, Concerning the Lawfulness and Unlawfulness of Plays," running to eighteen pages of small print. The prelims also contain a letter "To my Friend, the Author" signed "John Dryden."

254 "Scene *Verona*" (p. 1).

255 No authorial ascription on the title page, but Trotter signed the dedication. The prelims include four commendatory poems, three of them anonymous.

256 A commendatory poem by "Sylvius" was published in the prelims.

		Plays premiered in 1699				
Anon.[257]	Feign'd Friendship: or the Mad Reformer*†	No	[1699]	No	No	No	Ded; P/Ep
Anon. [William Penkethman?][258]	Love without Interest. A Comedy*†	Yes	1699	Yes	Yes	Yes	Ded; P/Ep[259]
J.C. [John Corye?][260]	A Cure for Jealousie. A Comedy†	Yes	1701	Yes	No	No	Ded; Loc; P/Ep
Abel Boyer (trans. Racine)	Achilles: or Iphigenia in Aulis. A Tragedy*†	Yes	1700	Yes	No	Yes	Ded; Pref; Loc; P/Ep
Colley Cibber (adapt. Shakespeare)[261]	The Tragical History of King Richard III.†	Yes	[1700]	Yes	No	Yes	Ded; Pref;[262]
Colley Cibber	Xerxes. A Tragedy†	Yes	1699	Yes	A bit	Yes	Ded; Loc; P/Ep
John Dennis	Iphigenia. A Tragedy†	Yes	1700	Yes	No	5 principals	Ded; Pref; Loc; P/Ep
Thomas Durfey	The Famous History and Fall of Massaniello, Parts I & II*†	Yes	1700 & 1699	Yes	Some	No	Ded; P/Ep (both parts)
George Farquhar	The Constant Couple. A Comedy*†	Yes	1699	Yes	Yes	Yes	Ded; Pref; Loc; P/Ep
Joseph Harris[263]	Love's a Lottery**†	Yes	1699	A bit	No	No	Ded; Loc; P;[264]

257 The unsigned dedication "To the Illustrious Prince James, Duke, Marquis, and Earl of Ormond, &c" says that it was put in the dedicator's care by the (unnamed) author.

258 A quirky, jokey dedication to more than thirty named men is signed "Will. Penkethman." It refers to the "indifferent Success and Reception of this short-liv'd Play."

259 With a second prologue "Designed to have been spoken by Mr Powell."

260 "J.C." is plausibly identified by Giles Jacob in 1719 in the "Addenda & Corrigenda" to his Poetical Register, p. 333, as the actor John Corey (fl. 1699–1735), a member of the Lincoln's Inn Fields company in 1699–1700.

261 Published with Shakespeare's words printed in italic type and thoughts indicated by single quotes ("'").

262 Lack of prologue and epilogue is highly unusual and extremely odd.

263 No ascription on the title page, but Harris signed the dedication, clearly speaking as the author.

264 The piece concludes with "A New Masque call'd Love and Riches Reconcil'd" in the place of an epilogue.

(cont.)

Playwright	Title (and genre if stated)	Publication year	List of characters	Connections explained	Characters described	Names of actors given	Other paratext
Charles Hopkins	*Friendship Improv'd. A Tragedy*‡†	1700	Yes	Yes	Only one	Yes	Ded; Loc; P/Ep
Peter Motteux (adapt. Fletcher)	*The Island Princess. Made into an Opera*[265]†	1699	Yes	A bit	A bit	Yes	Ded; To the Reader; Loc; P/Ep
Mary Pix	*The False Friend. A Tragedy*‡†	1699	Yes	Yes	No	Yes	Ded; Loc;[266] P/Ep
Henry Smith	*The Princess of Parma. A Tragedy*†	1699	Yes	Yes	Some	Yes	Loc; P/Ep

265 For a facsimile of British Library Add MS 15,318 (text and music), the separately published songs, and the 1699 edition of the text, see the reprint in the Music for London Entertainment series, Motteux, *The Island Princess*, Introduction by Price and Hume (1985).

266 The location specified is merely "A Hall."

Plays published in 1700

Playwright	Title (and genre if stated)	Publication year	List of characters	Connections explained	Characters described	Names of actors given	Other paratext
		Plays premiered in 1700					
Anon. [Charles Gildon?] (adapting Shakespeare)[267]	Measure for Measure*††	1700	Yes	Yes	Some	No	Ded; Loc; P/Ep
Anon. [John Vanbrugh] (adapting Fletcher)	The Pilgrim. A Comedy†[268]	1700	Yes	Yes	A bit	Yes	P/Ep[269]
Anon. [William Burnaby][270]	The Reform'd Wife. A Comedy[271]†	1700	Yes	Minimally	No	Yes	Pref; P/Ep
Susannah Centlivre[272]	The Perjur'd Husband. A Tragedy*†	1700	Yes	Yes	No	Yes	Ded; To the Reader; Loc; P/Ep

267 The title page reads "Written Originally by Mr. Shakespear: And now very much Alter'd; With Additions of several Entertainments of MUSICK.' The adaptation has been accepted without query as Charles Gildon's work by the editors of The London Stage (Part 1, p. 523) and virtually all other modern authorities, but the attribution seems to me dubious at best. So far as I know, it first appears in print in 1764 in David Erskine Baker's The Companion to the Play-House.

268 "Written Originally by Mr. Fletcher, and now very much Alter'd, with several Additions."

269 Contributed by John Dryden. Appended to the play is a twelve-page (separately paginated) "Dialogue, and Secular Masque, in the Pilgrim. Written by the Late Famous Mr. Dryden," duly puffed on the title page.

270 Though "Mr. Burnaby" was credited with four plays, including this one (his first) by "G.J." [Giles Jacob] as early as his The Poetical Register (1719), pp. 26, 285, he remained a very shadowy and ill-documented figure until the appearance of Budd's 1931 edition of The Dramatic Works of William Burnaby.

271 The "second edition" adds a new scene.

272 The title page has her maiden name, "S. Carroll."

Playwright	Title (and genre if stated)	Publication year	List of characters	Connections explained	Characters described	Names of actors given	Other paratext
Colley Cibber[273]	*Love makes a Man.* A Comedy*†	1701	Yes	Yes	A bit	Yes	Ded; Loc;[274] P/Ep;
William Congreve	*The Way of the World.* A Comedy†	1700	Yes	Yes	A bit	Yes	Ded; Loc; P/Ep
David Craufurd	*Courtship À la mode.* A Comedy†	1700	Yes	No	No	Yes	Ded; Pref; Loc; P/Ep
Francis Manning	*The Generous Choice.* A Comedy†	1700	Yes	Yes	A bit	No	Ded; Loc; P/Ep
John Oldmixon	*The Grove.* An Opera*†	1700	Yes	Yes	No	Yes	Ded; Pref; Loc; P/Ep
Mary Pix[275]	*The Beau Defeated.* A Comedy*†	[1700]	Yes	Yes	A bit	Yes	Ded; P/Ep
Nicholas Rowe	*The Ambitious Step-mother.* A Tragedy†	1701[276]	Yes	Yes	No	Yes	Ded; P/Ep
Thomas Southerne	*The Fate of Capua.* A Tragedy†	1700	Yes	No	No	Yes	Loc; P/Ep[277]
Catherine Trotter[278]	*Love at a Loss.* A Comedy*†	1701	Yes	Yes	A bit	Yes	Ded; P/Ep

273 A note following the dedication says, "If the Reader will please to look over *Fletcher's Elder Brother*, and his *Custom of the Country*, he may be satisfied how far I am oblig'd to those two Plays for part of this."

274 Location is specified as "Lisbon" at the start of Act III and is implied in the Dramatis Personae by the presence of the "Governour of Lisbon."

275 Authorship not credited on the title page, but Pix signed the dedication.

276 A "Second Edition" was published in 1702, "with the Addition of a New Scene," but in fact it contains no new scene. I offer the hypothesis that the scene arrived in time to get included in the first edition.

277 Lack of a dedication seems strange. Southerne was celebrated for his cultivation of patrons and huge profits from his benefits.

278 The title page reads "Written by the Author of the *Fatal Friendship*," and Trotter signed the dedication.

Bibliography

Astbury, Raymond, "The Renewal of the Licensing Act in 1693 and Its Lapse in 1695," *The Library*, series 5, 33.4 (December 1978), 296–322.

Avery, Emmett L., et al., *The London Stage, 1660–1800*, 11 vols. (Carbondale: Southern Illinois University Press, 1960–"1968" [1970]).

[Baker, David Erskine,] *The Companion to the Play-House*, 2 vols. (London: T. Becket et al., 1764).

Baker, Gerald, "The Name of Othello Is Not the Name of *Othello*," *Review of English Studies*, n.s. 67.1, no. 278 (2016), 62–78.

Barish, Jonas, *The Antitheatrical Prejudice* (Berkeley: University of California Press, 1981).

Bawcutt, N. W., ed., *The Control and Censorship of Caroline Drama: The Records of Sir Henry Herbert, Master of the Revels 1623–73* (Oxford: Oxford University Press, 1996).

Bentley, Gerald Eades, *The Profession of Player in Shakespeare's Time 1590–1642* (Princeton, NJ: Princeton University Press, 2014).

Berger, Thomas L., and Sonia Massai, with Tania Demetriou, ed., *Paratexts in English Printed Drama to 1642*, 2 vols. (Cambridge: Cambridge University Press, 2014).

Bond, David, "The Date of Richard Rhodes' *Flora's Vagaries*," *Philological Quarterly*, 65.3 (1986), 381–386.

Botica, Allan Richard, "Audience, Playhouse and Play in Restoration Theatre, 1660–1710," unpublished Oxford D.Phil thesis (1985 [1986]).

Cannan, Paul D., *The Emergence of Dramatic Criticism in England from Jonson to Pope* (London: Palgrave Macmillan, 2006).

Cibber, Colley, *An Apology for the Life of Mr. Colley Cibber Written by Himself*, ed. Robert W. Lowe, 2 vols. (London: John C. Nimmo, 1889).

Collier, Jeremy, *A Short View of the Immorality, and Profaneness of the English Stage* (London: S. Keble, R. Sare, H. Hindmarsh, 1698).

Covent Garden Drollery: A Miscellany of 1672, ed. G. Thorn-Drury (London: P. J. & A. E. Dobell, 1928).

Craig, Heidi C., "The King's Servants in Printed Paratexts, 1594–1695," *Huntington Library Quarterly*, 85:1 (Spring 2022), 151–69.

Crist, Timothy, "Government Control of the Press after the Expiration of the Printing Act in 1679," *Publishing History*, 5 (1979), 49–77.

Danchin, Pierre, ed., *The Prologues and Epilogues of the Restoration 1660–1700*, 7 vols. (Nancy: Publications Université Nancy II, 1981–8).

Depledge, Emma, "False Dating: The Case of the '1676' *Hamlet* Quartos," *Papers of the Bibliographical Society of America*, 112.2 (2018), 183–199.

Downes, John, *Roscius Anglicanus, or an Historical Review of the Stage* (1708), ed. Judith Milhous and Robert D. Hume (London: Society for Theatre Research, 1987).

Dryden, John, *The Letters of John Dryden*, ed. Charles E. Ward (Durham, NC: Duke University Press, 1942).

Dryden, John, *The Works of John Dryden*, gen. eds. H. T. Swedenberg, Jr., Vinton A. Dearing, et al. 20 vols. (Berkeley: University of California Press, 1956–2000).

Duffett, Thomas, *Three Burlesque Plays of Thomas Duffett*, ed. Ronald Eugene Lorenzo (Iowa City: University of Iowa Press, 1972).

Erne, Lukas, *Shakespeare and the Book Trade* (Cambridge: Cambridge University Press, 2013).

Ezell, Margaret J. M., *The Later Seventeenth Century, Volume 5 (1645–1714)*. The Oxford English Literary History (Oxford: Oxford University Press, 2017).

Genette, Gérard, *Paratexts: Thresholds of Interpretation*, trans. Jane E. Lewin (Cambridge: Cambridge University Press, 1997). Original French 1991.

[Gildon, Charles,] *The Lives and Characters of the English Dramatick Poets* (London: Thos. Leigh and William Turner [1699]).

Greg, W. W., *A Bibliography of the English Printed Drama to the Restoration*, 4 vols. (Oxford: Printed for the Bibliographical Society at the University Press, Oxford, 1939–1962).

Gurr, Andrew, *The Shakespearean Stage, 1574–1642*, 4th ed. (Cambridge: Cambridge University Press, 2009).

Harbage, Alfred, *Cavalier Drama* (New York: Modern Language Association, 1936).

Harbage, Alfred, *Annals of English Drama 975–1700* (Philadelphia: University of Pennsylvania Press 1940).

Harbage, Alfred, "Elizabethan–Restoration Palimpsest," *Modern Language Review*, 35.3 (1940), 287–319.

Haun, Eugene, *But Hark! More Harmony: The Libretti of Restoration Opera in English* (Ypsilanti: Eastern Michigan University Press, 1971).

Highfill, Philip H., Kalman A. Burnim, and Edward A. Langhans, *A Biographical Dictionary of Actors, Actresses, Musicians, Dancers, Managers & Other Stage Personnel in London, 1660–1800*, 16 vols. (Carbondale: Southern Illinois University Press, 1973–93).

Hughes, Derek, *English Drama, 1660–1700* (Oxford: Clarendon, 1996).

Hume, Robert D., *Dryden's Criticism* (Ithaca, NY: Cornell University Press, 1970).

Hume, Robert D., "The Date of Dryden's *Marriage A-la-Mode*," *Harvard Library Bulletin*, 21.2 (1973), 161–166.

Hume, Robert D., *The Development of English Drama in the Late Seventeenth Century* (Oxford: Clarendon, 1976). [Hume 1976a]

Hume, Robert D., "The Date of Mountfort's *The Life and Death of Doctor Faustus*," *Archiv für das Studium der Neueren Sprachen*, 213 (1976), 109–111. [Hume 1976b]

Hume, Robert D., "The Satiric Design of Nat. Lee's *The Princess of Cleve*," *Journal of English and Germanic Philology*, 75 (1976), 117–138. [Hume 1976c]

Hume, Robert D., "The Dorset Garden Theatre: A Review of Facts and Problems," *Theatre Notebook*, 33 (1979), 4–17.

Hume, Robert D., "Securing a Repertory: Plays on the London Stage 1660–5," in *Poetry and Drama 1570–1700: Essays in Honour of Harold F. Brooks*, ed. Antony Coleman and Antony Hammond (London: Methuen, 1981), pp. 156–172.

Hume, Robert D., "The Nature of the Dorset Garden Theatre," *Theatre Notebook*, 36 (1982), 99–109.

Hume, Robert D., *The Rakish Stage: Studies in English Drama, 1660–1800* (Carbondale: Southern Illinois University Press, 1983).

Hume, Robert D., *Reconstructing Contexts: The Aims and Principles of Archaeo-historicism* (Oxford: Clarendon, 1999). [Hume 1999a]

Hume, Robert D., "Jeremy Collier and the Future of the London Theater in 1698," *Studies in Philology*, 96 (1999), 480–511. [Hume 1999b]

Hume, Robert D., "*Feniza or The Ingeniouse Mayde*: A 'Lost' Carolean Comedy Found – and a Source for Shadwell's *The Amorous Bigotte*," *English Manuscript Studies, 1100–1700*, 18 (2013), 68–103.

Hume, Robert D., "The Value of Money in Eighteenth-Century England: Incomes, Prices, Buying Power – and Some Problems in Cultural Economics," *Huntington Library Quarterly*, 77.4 (2014), 373–416.

Hume, Robert D., "Theatre Performance Records in London, 1660–1705," *Review of English Studies*, n.s. 67.3, no. 280 (2016), 468–495.

Hume, Robert D., "*The London Stage, 1660–1800*: A Short History, Retrospective Anatomy, and Projected Future," *Electronic British Library Journal*, 2022 articles.

Hume, Robert D., "Annotation in Scholarly Editions of Plays: Problems, Options, and Principles," in *Notes on Footnotes: Annotating Eighteenth-Century Literature*, ed. Melvyn New and Anthony W. Lee. Penn State

Series in the History of the Book (University Park: Pennsylvania State University Press, 2023).

Hume, Robert D., "The Strange Anonymity of John Vanbrugh," *Huntington Library Quarterly*, forthcoming.

Jacob, Giles, *The Poetical Register: Or, The Lives and Characters of the English Dramatick Poets. With an Account of Their Writings* (London: E. Curll, 1719).

Kewes, Paulina, *Authorship and Appropriation: Writing for the Stage in England, 1660–1710* (Oxford: Clarendon, 1998).

Kewes, Paulina, "[A] Play, Which I Presume to Call *Original*': Appropriation, Creative Genius, and Eighteenth-Century Playwriting," *Studies in the Literary Imagination*, 34.1 (Spring 2001), 17–47.

Keymer, Thomas, *Poetics of the Pillory: English Literature and Seditious Libel, 1660–1820* (Oxford: Oxford University Press, 2019).

Kitchin, George, *Sir Roger L'Estrange: A Contribution to the History of the Press in the Seventeenth Century* (London: Kegan Paul, Trench, Trubner & Company, Ltd., 1913).

Lancaster, H. Carrington, *The Comédie Française, 1680–1701: Plays, Actors, Spectators, Finances* (Baltimore, MD: Johns Hopkins University Press, 1941).

Langbaine, Gerard, *An Account of the English Dramatick Poets* (Oxford: LL. For George West and Henry Clements, 1691).

Langhans, Edward A., "A Conjectural Reconstruction of the Dorset Garden Theatre," *Theatre Survey*, 13.2 (1972), 74–93.

Langhans, Edward A., *Restoration Promptbooks* (Carbondale: Southern Illinois University Press, 1981).

Lee, Nathaniel, *The Works of Nathaniel Lee*, 2 vols., ed. Thomas B. Stroup and Arthur L. Cooke (1954–5; rpt. Metuchen, NJ, Scarecrow Reprint Corporation, 1968).

Lincoln, Stoddard, "John Eccles: The Last of a Tradition," D.Phil. Thesis, Wadham College, Oxford University, 1963.

Love, Harold, "Who Were the Restoration Audience?" *Yearbook of English Studies*, 10 (1980), 21–44.

"M, W", *The Female Wits: or, the Triumvirate of Poets at Rehearsal. A Comedy*, facsimile of the 1704 Edition, with Introduction by Lucyle Hook (Los Angeles, CA: Augustan Reprint Society, 1967).

Maguire, Nancy Klein, *Regicide and Restoration: English Tragicomedy, 1660–1671* (Cambridge: Cambridge University Press, 1992).

Milhous, Judith, "Thomas Betterton's Playwriting," *Bulletin of the New York Public Library*, 77 (1974), 375–392.

Milhous, Judith, "Company Management," in *The London Theatre World, 1660–1800*, ed. Robert D. Hume (Carbondale: Southern Illinois University Press, 1980), chapter 1.

Milhous, Judith, and Robert D. Hume, "Dating Play Premières from Publication Data, 1660–1700," *Harvard Library Bulletin*, 22.4 (1974), 374–405.

Milhous, Judith, and Robert D. Hume, "Attribution Problems in English Drama, 1660–1700," *Harvard Library Bulletin*, 31.1 (1983), 5–39.

Milhous, Judith, and Robert D. Hume, *Producible Interpretation: Eight English Plays, 1675–1707* (Carbondale: Southern Illinois University Press, 1985).

Milhous, Judith, and Robert D. Hume, "Charles Killigrew's Petition about the Master of the Revels' Power As Censor (1715)," *Theatre Notebook*, 41 (1987), 74–79.

Milhous, Judith, and Robert D. Hume, "Playwrights' Remuneration in Eighteenth-Century London," special issue of *Harvard Library Bulletin*, n. s. 10.2–3 (1999), 3–90.

Milhous, Judith, and Robert D. Hume, *The Publication of Plays in London, 1660–1800* (London: The British Library, 2015).

Nicoll, Allardyce, *A History of English Drama 1660–1900*, 6 vols., rev. ed. (Cambridge: Cambridge University Press, 1965).

O'Donnell, Mary Ann, *Aphra Behn: An Annotated Bibliography of Primary and Secondary Sources*, 2nd ed. (Aldershot: Ashgate, 2004).

Oxford Dictionary of National Biography, ed. H. C. G. Matthew and Brian Harrison, 60 vols. (Oxford: Oxford University Press, 2004).

Pepys, Samuel, *The Diary of Samuel Pepys*, ed. Robert Latham and William Matthews, 11 vols. (London: Bell, 1970–83).

Philips, Katherine, *Letters from Orinda to Poliarchus* (London: W. B. for Bernard Lintott, 1705).

Randall, Dale B. J., *Winter Fruit: English Drama 1642–1660* (Lexington: University Press of Kentucky, 1995).

Reed, Isaac, *Biographia Dramatica, or, A Companion to the Playhouse*, 2 vols. (London: Rivington et al., 1782).

Schoenbaum, S[amuel], ed. (revising Harbage), *Annals of English Drama 975–1700*, 2nd edition (London: Methuen, 1964).

Shadwell, Thomas, *The Complete Works of Thomas Shadwell*, ed. Montague Summers, 5 vols. (London: Fortune Press, 1927).

Smith, Helen, and Louise Wilson, eds., *Renaissance Paratexts* (Cambridge: Cambridge University Press, 2011).

Solomon, Diana, *Prologues and Epilogues of Restoration Theater: Gender and Comedy, Performance and Print* (Newark: University of Delaware Press, 2013).

Treadwell, Michael, "The Stationers and the Printing Acts at the End of the Seventeenth Century," in *The Cambridge History of the Book in Britain, Vol. IV: 1557–1695*, ed. John Barnard and Donald F. McKenzie with the assistance of Maureen Bell (Cambridge: Cambridge University Press, 2002), pp. 755–776.

Vander Motten, J. P., *Sir William Killigrew (1606–1695): His Life and Dramatic Works* (Gent: Rijksuniversiteit te Gent, 1980).

Vander Motten, J. P., and Joseph S. Johnston Jr., "Sir William Killigrew's Unpublished Revisions of *The Seege of Urbin*," *The Library*, series 6, 5.2 (1983), 159–165.

Vareschi, Mark, and Mattie Burkert, "Archives, Numbers, Meaning: The Eighteenth-Century Playbill at Scale," *Theatre Journal*, 68.4 (2016), 597–613.

Wagonheim, Sylvia Stoler, *Annals of English Drama 975–1700*, 3rd edition [revising Harbage and Schoenbaum] (London: Routledge, 1989).

White, Arthur F., *John Crowne: His Life and Dramatic Works* (Cleveland, OH: Western Reserve University Press, 1922).

White, Arthur F., "The Office of Revels and Dramatic Censorship during the Restoration Period," *Western Reserve University Bulletin*, n.s. 34 (1931), 5–45.

Wiley, Autrey Nell, ed., *Rare Prologues and Epilogues 1642–1700* (London: G. Allen and Unwin, 1940).

Wilson, John, *John Wilson's The Cheats*, ed. Milton C. Nahm. From the MS. in the Library of Worcester College, Oxford (Oxford: Basil Blackwell, 1935).

Wood, Anthony à, *Athenæ Oxonienses: An Exact History of All the Writers and Bishops Who Have Had Their Education in the University of Oxford*, rev. ed. Philip Bliss, 4 vols. (London: F. C. and J. Rivington, et al., 1813–20).

Cambridge Elements ☰

Eighteenth-Century Connections

Series Editors

Eve Tavor Bannet
University of Oklahoma

Eve Tavor Bannet is George Lynn Cross Professor Emeritus, University of Oklahoma and editor of *Studies in Eighteenth-Century Culture*. Her monographs include *Empire of Letters: Letter Manuals and Transatlantic Correspondence 1688–1820* (Cambridge, 2005), *Transatlantic Stories and the History of Reading, 1720–1820* (Cambridge, 2011), and *Eighteenth-Century Manners of Reading: Print Culture and Popular Instruction in the Anglophone Atlantic World* (Cambridge, 2017). She is editor of *British and American Letter Manuals 1680–1810* (Pickering & Chatto, 2008), *Emma Corbett* (Broadview, 2011) and, with Susan Manning, *Transatlantic Literary Studies* (Cambridge, 2012).

Markman Ellis
Queen Mary University of London

Markman Ellis is Professor of Eighteenth-Century Studies at Queen Mary University of London. He is the author of *The Politics of Sensibility: Race, Gender and Commerce in the Sentimental Novel* (1996), *The History of Gothic Fiction* (2000), *The Coffee-House: a Cultural History* (2004), and *Empire of Tea* (co-authored, 2015). He edited *Eighteenth-Century Coffee-House Culture* (4 vols, 2006) and *Tea and the Tea-Table in Eighteenth-Century England* (4 vols 2010), and co-editor of *Discourses of Slavery and Abolition* (2004) and *Prostitution and Eighteenth-Century Culture: Sex, Commerce and Morality* (2012).

Advisory Board

Linda Bree, *Independent*
Claire Connolly, *University College Cork*
Gillian Dow, *University of Southampton*
James Harris, *University of St Andrews*
Thomas Keymer, *University of Toronto*
Jon Mee, *University of York*
Carla Mulford, *Penn State University*
Nicola Parsons, *University of Sydney*
Manushag Powell, *Purdue University*
Robbie Richardson, *University of Kent*
Shef Rogers, *University of Otago*
Eleanor Shevlin, *West Chester University*
David Taylor, *Oxford University*
Chloe Wigston Smith, *University of York*
Roxann Wheeler, *Ohio State University*
Eugenia Zuroski, *MacMaster University*

About the Series

Exploring connections between verbal and visual texts and the people, networks, cultures and places that engendered and enjoyed them during the long Eighteenth Century, this innovative series also examines the period's uses of oral, written and visual media, and experiments with the digital platform to facilitate communication of original scholarship with both colleagues and students.

Cambridge Elements ≡

Eighteenth-Century Connections

Elements in the Series